winning
karate

Joseph Jennings

Contemporary Books, Inc.
Chicago

Library of Congress Cataloging in Publication Data

Jennings, Joseph.
   Winning karate.

   Includes index.
   1. Karate—I. Title.
GV1114.3.J46   796.8'153   81-71086
ISBN 0-8092-5723-8 (cloth)   AACR2
ISBN 0-8092-5800-5 (pbk.)

Copyright © 1982 by Joseph Jennings
All rights reserved
Published by Contemporary Books, Inc.
180 North Michigan Avenue, Chicago, Illinois 60601
Manufactured in the United States of America
Library of Congress Catalog Card Number: 81-71086
International Standard Book Number: 0-8092-5723-8 (cloth)
                           0-8092-5800-5 (paper)

Published simultaneously in Canada by
Beaverbooks, Ltd.
150 Lesmill Road
Don Mills, Ontario M3B 2T5
Canada

To my wonderful parents,
Tracy and Florence Jennings

contents

Okinawan Master Angi Uezu, 7th Dan, Isshin Ryu Karate-Do.

preface

Karate is an addictive art. Its thousands of practitioners throughout the world can attest to that. Once experienced, it has a way of becoming a lifelong dedication. This dedication stems from the many challenges karate has to offer each practitioner.

I am often asked by people wishing to get involved in the martial arts which type of karate is the best to study. Although there are over one hundred different styles in the world today, no one traditional system rates superior to the others. You must always remember: It is never the style that makes one a self-defense expert or a national champion, but the hard work and dedication of the student coupled with the expertise of a good instructor.

In this book I have touched on the many factors that make up the art of karate, which you are sure to experience throughout your training. Although volumes could be written on each factor, I have zeroed in on the most important points that will give you an immediate understanding of the mechanics that go into the execution of certain techniques, and will help you develop a greater knowledge of karate in general.

Written in the same easy-to-understand manner in which I instruct students at my academies, this book presents only those techniques proven effective time and again in training and competition. This is not to imply that my techniques are the only ones appropriate for the encounters shown. Although I am a practitioner of the traditional Okinawan, Isshin Ryu Karate system, I am always open-minded about the use of alternative techniques that other systems and martial artists have to offer. The reader should be open-minded, too.

By training no less than three days per week, the novice will be capable of mastering basic blocks, kicks, punches, and stances, while intermediate and advanced students will be able to gain new insight into ways of improving their competitive sparring and kata skills.

Since the book's theories and techniques can be applied to any style of karate, I feel instructors will find *Winning Karate* a valuable teaching aid for their classes.

In closing, I would like to mention that one should never underestimate the destructive power of the techniques put forth in this book. I hope everyone who studies from it will exercise control and restraint. Only use karate as a last resort. A true karate practitioner lives by the following: "When your hand goes out withdraw your anger; when your anger goes out withdraw your hand." (Okinawan Proverb)

chapter one

basic principles

Although the origin of karate (meaning "empty hand") is over 1,000 years old with early beginnings in China and Okinawa, it did not find its way to American soil until the early '50s. The people most responsible for introducing karate to the American public were United States' servicemen stationed overseas in such countries as Okinawa, Japan, and Korea. During their stay, many of the GIs who took an interest in the martial arts were fortunate enough to study under some of the greatest karate masters that ever lived. Upon returning to the states, they formed karate clubs at local YMCAs, community centers, and makeshift home gyms, thus planting the seeds for karate's future growth.

Today, with many top American and Oriental instructors

teaching throughout the country, karate now enjoys the same popularity and status that many other American sporting activities do.

IMPORTANT POINTS

Before we begin our journey into the world's most sophisticated and deadly self-defense art, one must first understand the underlying principles that all karate techniques are built on. Mastery of karate can only be achieved by applying these important points to every aspect of your training:

Breath control and kiai. To develop exceptional reflexes and blinding speed, the body must be in a relaxed, alert state prior to the execution of a block, punch, or kick. A constantly tense posture will sap your energy and slow your movements. The only time the muscles should tense is upon impact, for the purpose of creating greater power and stability. Tensing of the body also protects it against the force of a possible counterstrike by your opponent. Proper breathing technique is performed by exhaling air out of the mouth from the lower abdomen when executing a technique. Not on all strikes, but occasionally a loud shout or *kiai* (as it is referred to in Japanese) should be employed.

The kiai serves many important functions. When properly timed it can be used as a feint to upset your opponent's guard and leave openings for your attack. Psychologically, it increases your strength, courage, and fighting spirit.

There is a documented story of an old master who, while meditating in the mountains, was attacked by a tiger. As the tiger charged, the master rooted himself in a deep stance and kiaied with such fierceness that the big cat stopped dead in his tracks, turned, and ran into the woods in search of easier prey. The kiai can have the same effect on a would-be attacker.

The kiai should not be a scream, but rather a deep, loud, and

2

abrupt sound. In training, kiais are executed on the last strike in a series of techniques and used to emphasize major movements in the *katas* (forms).

Kiai

Improper focusing and loss of power is caused by hitting only the surface of the intended target.

Always focus your technique at a point four inches beyond the target for ultimate power.

Focus point. To focus is to concentrate all your force into the target at the instant contact is made. Proper focusing gives the *karateka* (student) the power to smash through stacks of bricks or the ability to stop an attacker with one blow. Although many karate practitioners execute their techniques with damaging force, few strike with 100 percent of their total strength because they focus incorrectly. Ultimate force is achieved by striking at an imaginary point four inches beyond your intended target. For example, if you wish to hit your attacker in the nose, your target should not be the tip of the nose, but an imaginary point near the back of the head. This will avoid weak, ineffective surface hitting and cause much greater damage. Focusing beyond your target also helps compensate if your opponent moves back and tries to roll with the punch.

By adjusting your focus point, you also can learn to pull and control your strikes. For example, in point fighting contests, where hard face contact is not allowed, you can mentally focus your strike to stop at a point two inches in front of your opponent's head. Through experience, you will be amazed at how well you can control fullpower strikes in training and competition.

Speed is power. Striking with effective power and focus can only be achieved by executing techniques with great speed. Speed is what gives a smaller person the ability to hit like a heavyweight. In training, always strive to improve the speed of your techniques; you will never be lacking in effective power.

Form. Good form exemplifies the beauty of karate. From the basics to advanced techniques, you can immediately tell the difference between a mediocre performance and an outstanding one by a practitioner's form. Proper form can only be achieved by executing each karate technique with peak concentration. Good form also increases the effectiveness of your strike . . . always strive for perfection.

Timing. Outstanding karate technique is worthless unless it can be delivered with perfect timing. Timing is the ability to move

This fighter shows perfect timing as he catches his opponent with a side kick to the midsection.

5

the moment your opponent is at his weakest, when his concentration is broken and he is off guard. It also is the ability to know what your opponent will do before he moves. Masters call it a sixth sense. Regardless, timing is developed by training with a variety of different opponents, and improved upon through experience.

Spirit. Karate, in part, is an art of imagination. Hundreds of techniques are executed in training against opponents who don't exist. To give more power and meaning to your routines, you must always imagine the attacker you are in combat with. By training with this vision, you will develop a positive fighting spirit, which is needed to be victorious in competition and in self-defense.

A positive, fighting spirit is essential to being victorious in competition.

Meditation is performed before and after each class as a means of helping students concentrate more intensely.

Meditation. Performed before and after every class, meditation helps the student to concentrate by eliminating thoughts that do not pertain to karate. Assume a formal, seated position by sitting erect on the insteps of your feet. Then inhale through the nose, down to the lower abdomen, and out the mouth. Each breath should be done slowly and fully. Usually an instructor will keep time of inhaling and exhaling. Keeping the eyes closed, imagine yourself performing karate techniques with exceptional form and skill. A good mental image can greatly enhance your physical performance.

Belt ranks. Since I will refer to the various belt ranks of karate throughout this book, I feel it is very important to mention them before we start. Using my school's promotion system as an example, different colored belt ranks are commonly presented in the following order: white, yellow, orange, green, brown, and

7

black. Each belt is presented when a student reaches a new level of proficiency and has completed special requirements. Although each student is different, the average training time for each belt is as follows: Yellow—three months (beginner), Orange—seven months (intermediate), Green—one year (advanced), Brown—three years (advanced), and Black—five years (advanced instructor). There are ten degrees of black belt, which are awarded at various times for a student's contributions to the art. A red belt is presented after fifty years of continuous training and dedication. Only a handful of masters in the world wear them.

Karate bow (rei). The bow used in karate is an oriental gesture of respect and courtesy. The *rei* is performed whenever going on or off the training area, and to acknowledge the presence of the head instructor. You may use it to show respect to a training partner or a competitor. In competition, the bow also signifies the beginning and end of a free fighting match. Correct bowing is performed by keeping the heels together, toes out at a 45-degree angle, and head tilted up as you bow, keeping your eyes on your opponent, real or imagined.

Karate Bow (Rei)

Weight Training

There probably isn't a sport today that hasn't felt the influence of weight training on improving an athlete's performance. Karate is no exception. More and more karate studios are incorporating weight-lifting equipment into their programs to help the martial artist gain greater strength, speed, endurance, and flexibility. Even ancient masters understood the value of resistance training. They regularly included the lifting of heavy stones and logs into their workouts to increase striking power. I'm a strong believer in using weights as a way to improve a karateka's performance. At the end of Chapters 4 and 5, I have included weight training exercises I feel to be an invaluable adjunct to regular karate training. They concentrate on strengthening specific body parts such as the arms, chest, back, and shoulders for blocking and punching, and the thighs and thigh biceps for kicking. The added strength gained from the use of weights has often helped my students in dealing with heavier opponents in sparring competition.

When training with weights, you need train only two days per week to greatly increase your power, without taking away from your karate workouts. For achieving maximum results you should have access to a well-equipped gym that includes the basic leg, arm, and back machines along with a variety of free weights. By keeping a regular weekly routine, your karate technique is sure to excel.

The only way one can benefit from a weight routine is to train consistently. Be sure to have a three-day span between workouts to give the body time to rest and recuperate. When performing weight training routines, do the entire body in one day by completing the upper-body exercises first, then ending with the legs. For each body part to benefit the most, perform all the sets of each exercise one after the other, resting no more than one minute between sets. Perform the exercises in the exact order shown. Do no less than eight repetitions for each exercise using a weight that will make you strain to finish the last two repetitions. Although I advocate three sets for most exercises, as a beginner you may want to start with two and build up to three as your strength and endurance increase.

chapter two

flexibility training

Being "loose," as it is commonly referred to in karate training, means being flexible. Flexibility training is vital for warming up the body and for achieving a high degree of proficiency in your kicking techniques. It also is an important factor in the prevention of pulled muscles, tendons, and ligaments. The less resistance a leg has to tightness, the greater speed, power, and accuracy it will have.

Although you may never achieve a full leg split, everyone, no matter what age, is capable of greatly improving his or her flexibility over a period of time by following a daily stretching routine.

Besides performing stretching exercises alone, you should make it a point to stretch regularly with a partner. I find students can achieve greater flexibility this way because the help of an assistant enables them to stretch beyond what normally could be achieved alone.

THE STRETCHING EXERCISES

The areas of the body that most affect one's kicking abilities are the hamstring, groin, hips, and back muscles. The following exercises are specifically designed to give greater flexibility to these areas. With a partner, perform all of the following exercises two times each and no less than four days a week in the exact order shown. Both people should complete each exercise before going on to the next. It is very important to inform your partner about how much pull and pressure your body can handle while being stretched. Hold the stretched position from 10 to 60 seconds depending on your physical ability.

KEY POINTS TO FOLLOW WHEN STRETCHING

1. Make it a point to stretch no less than 10 minutes before and 10 minutes after each training session.
2. Never force a stretch or an injury is likely to occur. Begin by slowly stretching to the point where you cannot stretch any further. At this point, hold your stretched position for 10 seconds, keeping the body in a relaxed state. Break from the stretched position for 10 seconds, then assume the same position for another 10 seconds trying to stretch a little further each time. As your stretch improves, hold for longer periods.
3. Do not bounce when stretching. Bouncing acts in a negative way, by actually tightening the muscles instead of loosening them.
4. When stretching, you should not be in any great pain. Stretching should feel good and be something you look forward

to. Do not get discouraged with your level of flexibility. Some people are born with great stretch, while others have to work very hard to attain theirs. Be patient; I've seen students who could not touch their toes go on to become exceptional kickers through intensive flexibility training. Achieving great flexibility is a long process and cannot be achieved overnight.

5. After completing a stretching routine do not immediately begin throwing full-powered kicks. Spend a few minutes executing light kicking and punching combinations to complete warming up the entire body.

PALMS TO FLOOR. Stand with your feet together, knees straight, and hands open on your hips, with palms facing upward.

Bend down as far as possible, keeping the knees straight at all times, and try to touch your palms to the floor.

13

BACK STRETCH. Facing your partner, stand with your feet together, holding each other's arms near the elbows.

Bend down as far as possible, keeping the knees and back straight with the head held up.

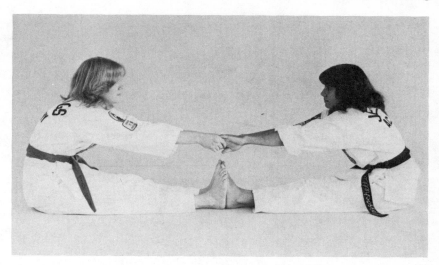

LEG PULL. Sit facing your partner with the soles of your feet touching together and with hands clutched.

Slowly pull your partner forward as far as possible.

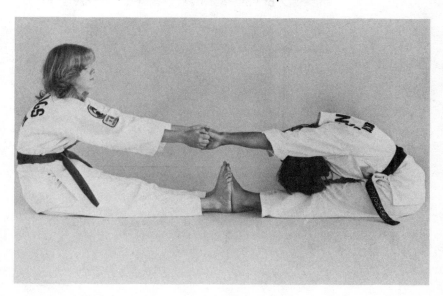

BACK TO BACK. Sitting back to back, lock your arms with each other, keeping the legs together and knees straight.

Slowly walk up the back of your partner, bending her forward.

16

KNEE STAND. With your partner behind you, sit with your feet together and legs pulled into the groin area. Hold your feet with your hands.

Keeping your hands on your partner's shoulders, carefully stand on one knee.

Complete the stretch by standing on the other knee. Regulate the amount of pressure you wish to apply by keeping your hands on the shoulders.

SADDLE STRETCH. In a seated position, open your partner's legs as wide as they will go, keeping your feet just below the knees, holding each other's arms.

Slowly lean back, pulling your partner forward.

18

flexibility training

BUTTERFLY SPLIT. With your partner on her back, stand in front, holding her legs up.

Begin slowly to push your partner's legs apart, holding them at the calf area. At this point, butt your knees up against your partner's legs to keep them from falling forward.

Complete the butterfly split by pushing the legs apart as far as they will go. The person being stretched must keep knees locked and feet in the blade position.

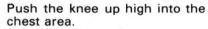

FULL SPLIT. With your partner behind you, split out on your heels as far down as possible.

Slowly push down on the hips, completing the split.

KNEE PUSH. Stand against a wall with the knee up and toes pointed down.

Push the knee up high into the chest area.

FRONT LEG STRETCH. Stand with your back against a wall and with your partner holding your leg up at waist height.

SIDE KICK STRETCH. Stand sideways with your shoulder against the wall. Keeping your leg straight and foot in the blade position, have your partner hold your leg at waist height directly to your side.

Keeping the knee straight and toes pulled back, slowly push your partner's leg straight up toward the wall.

Slowly raise the leg toward the wall as high as it will go.

chapter three

stances

The development of proper balance is the most important factor in acquiring strong blocking, kicking, and punching techniques. A strong foundation comes from a variety of karate stances, each uniquely developed for the execution of certain offensive and defensive strikes. Some karate stances also act as an excellent leg-strengthening exercise. One need only stand in the horse stance position for two or more minutes to feel the tiring effect it will have on the thigh muscles.

Although perfect stance form is stressed in training, this may not always be the case in self-defense or sparring situations. For example, if you are surprised by your attacker, you may not have time to set in a picture-perfect stance. You should not worry about this happening, because the tremendous sense of balance one acquires in karate training will compensate, enabling you to deliver effective strikes even if caught off guard.

In training, try not to favor one stance over the other. This can be dangerous because you may find youself in a situation where you cannot use your favorite stance effectively. A good karateka is versatile, able to adapt a variety of stances to any situation.

Though there are as many as fourteen different karate stances, the following five are the most practical and most commonly used.

Front Stance

Used most often in basic drills and kata training, the front stance is usually the first posture a student will learn. Other stances are taught after mastery of this stance. Assume this stance by keeping one leg back and positioning your feet so the

FRONT STANCE. Front view.   Side view.

inside edge of your foot lines up with the outside edge of your shoulders. Keep your feet pointed forward with your upper-body weight distributed evenly on each leg and with the knees slightly bent.

Horse Stance

This was the dominant offensive and defensive stance used by American tournament fighters of the late '60s and early '70s. By facing your opponent sideways, you offer few vulnerable targets. Stand with your legs wide apart, lining up the outside edge of your heels with your elbows. Squat your upper-body weight down, keeping your feet turned out at 45-degree angles. Keep your body weight distributed evenly on each leg.

HORSE STANCE. Front view.   **Side view.**

Cat Stance

Given its name because of its resemblance to a cat's striking posture, the cat stance is performed by turning your rear foot completely sideways and placing 90 percent of your body weight on it. At a 90-degree angle to your rear foot, place your front foot high on the ball with the remaining 10 percent of your weight. Both shoulders should be facing the front with your hands in a guard position. All the weight is shifted to the rear leg so the front can quickly kick out to the groin, knee, or solar plexus. The cat stance is an excellent posture for close encounters.

CAT STANCE. Front view.   **Side view.**

Leaning Back Stance

This stance is used strictly as a defensive stance. Keeping your legs wide apart with your feet parallel to each other at 45-degree angles, lean 70 percent of your body weight on the back leg and 30 percent on the front. (Your front leg is the outstretched leg.) Your upper body must be kept sideways with the head leaning back, out of your opponent's reach. The front arm should be down covering your rib cage. This stance leaves few vulnerable areas. If attacked, the front leg is used to deliver defensive side and back kicks.

LEANING BACK STANCE.
Front view.   Side view.

American Free Fighting Stance

Uniquely American, this stance was evolved in the middle '70s by American semicontact fighters who found the traditional Japanese horse stance restricting. By keeping the feet closer together and by standing more erect, they were able to achieve greater mobility and speed. The higher stance also enabled them to execute techniques with less chance of telegraphing their moves, which often occurs in competition when fighting from a low stance. Assume this stance by facing your opponent sideways. Keep your feet at 45-degree angles and shoulders' width apart, knees slightly bent, and with your body weight distributed evenly on each leg. Besides being a versatile free fighting stance, it also is an excellent self-defense posture.

FREE FIGHTING STANCE.

ALTERNATING STANCES

When alternating from stance to stance, it is of utmost importance to move in a cautious and protective manner to avoid being left vulnerable to a counterattack. To accomplish this, the following technique must be applied to any stance maneuvers. Using the front stance as an example, begin moving forward by stepping in a half circle, bringing your back leg in toward the supporting foot, then out to complete the stance.

As stated earlier, a completed front stance should have one leg back and both feet pointing forward, with the inside edge of the foot directly in line with the outside edge of your shoulder. Bringing the leg in when moving helps protect the groin and midsection against a possible counterattack. When moving back or retreating, the same half-circle motion applies. When shifting

A

B

C   D

stances, keep your back straight and head up, and alternate your guard accordingly.

A proper *guard* should have the front leg hand held high to protect the ribs, with the back hand held low around the waist, protecting the stomach and solar plexus. Practice all your stances by performing them up and down the training hall floor.

KEY POINTS TO DEVELOPING A STRONG STANCE

1. Simply assuming a karate stance does not mean one will have a strong sense of balance. To avoid being easily knocked over one must understand how to set properly by applying the following points, which pertain to all stances.

    A. Always keep the knees slightly bent for greater mobility.

    B. Grip the ground with your toes.

    C. Lightly concentrate your body weight down to the ground as if someone were pushing straight down on your shoulders.

When set properly in your stance, your partner should have a hard time lifting you off the ground.

By applying these three factors to your stances, you will no longer be just standing there; you will be planted to the ground like a brick wall.

To get a better idea of how much stronger these techniques can make your stance, assume the front stance without applying points A, B, and C, and have a friend of equal body weight lift you off the ground. By placing his hands around your waist, your partner should be able to lift you with little effort. Now set in the same stance by applying points A, B, and C. Your body weight will seem to have doubled as your friend strains to lift you.

2. When shifting stances, do not drop your guard position, leaving openings to the midsection and chest area. Alternate your guard accordingly.

3. Regardless of the stance you take, you should always be able to block, kick, and punch effectively. If you are unable to perform any of these techniques, your balance is off, and you must make the proper adjustments immediately.

4. At all times keep the back straight and head up, as if balancing a glass of water on top of it. Always look at your opponent's throat area, never at the ground or intended target. This will prevent him from anticipating your point-of-attack.

5. Be firm in your stance, yet keep your shoulders and arms relaxed for greater speed.

6. Check your stance form by practicing regularly in a full-length mirror.

chapter four

hands of steel

HAND WEAPONS

The hands of a karate practitioner can be formed into a variety of weapons, each suited for striking different vital areas. They are as follows:

Forefist

To make the proper fist, start with the hand fully open. Close all four fingers tightly, then place the thumb on top lying it flat on its side. Keep the fist tight at all times as if trying to crush a golf ball. For greater destructive force, contact should be made only with the two large top knuckles. Also, when striking, make certain the wrist is perfectly straight, keeping the bones in line upon impact. Target areas for the *seiken* (forefist punch) include the solar plexus, groin, ribs, nose, and jaw.

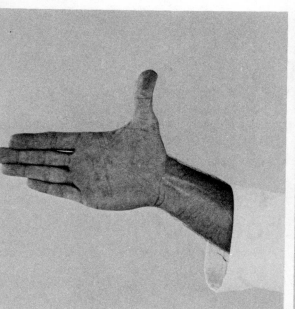

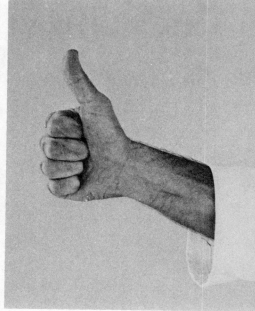

34

hands of steel

Front view.

Forefist applied.

Backfist

Make the same exact fist position as that of the forefist. The *uraken* (backfist strike) is made by hitting with the back of the hand.

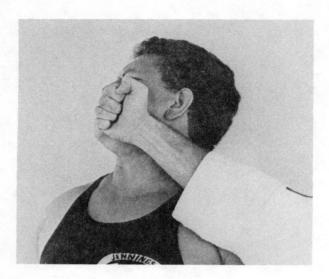

Palm Heel

Pull all your fingers back with the thumb tucked in. The *teisho* (palm heel) is an ideal weapon for hitting the attacker under the jaw or nose.

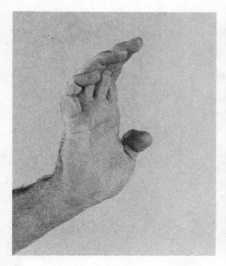

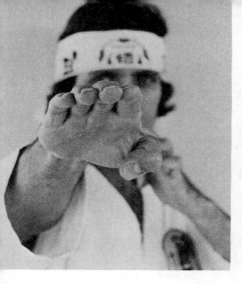 

Spear Hand

Hold the hand open with the thumb down. Tense the fingers and slightly bend them in. A devastating weapon, the *nukite* (spear hand) is used to strike soft areas such as the throat, groin, solar plexus, or eyes.

Hammer Fist

Make the basic karate fist and strike by coming directly down on your opponent with the underside of your hand. Target areas for the *kentsui* (hammer fist) include the nose, collar bone, and elbow.

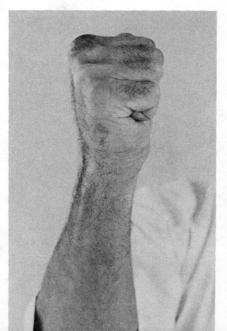 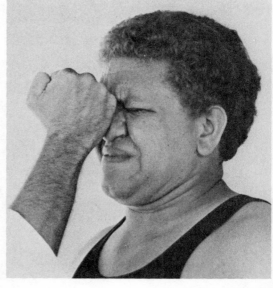

Knife Hand

The side of the hand is made the same way as the spear hand position, but instead of striking with the fingertips, contact is made with the side of the hand. The *shuto* (knife hand) strike is delivered straight down, and across to the ribs, neck, temples, jaw, kidneys, or elbows.

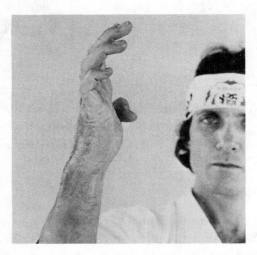

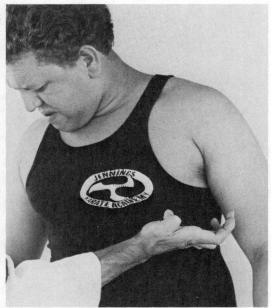

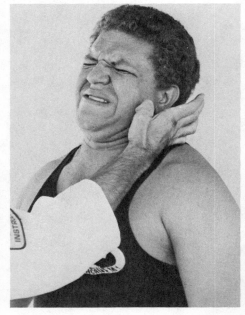

Claw Hand

Make the *toho* (claw hand) by keeping the fingers together and thumb out, creating an arch in the hand. Strike by thrusting the palm into the throat for choking.

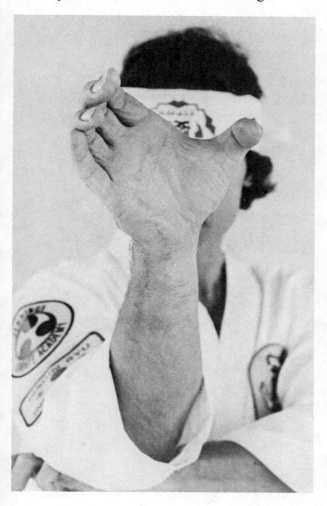

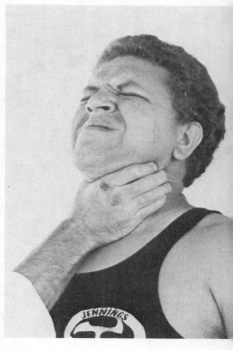

Ridge Hand

This strike, the *haito,* is the reverse of the knife hand. With the hand in the same position as the knife hand, strike by making contact with the inside edge of the hand. The haito's primary targets include the ribs, temples, jaw, throat, and solar plexus.

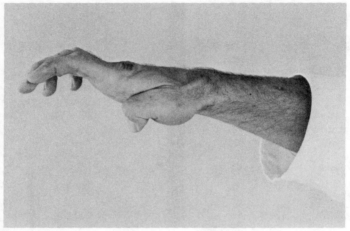

Elbow

Karate's most destructive upper body weapon, the *empi* (elbow) is an excellent weapon for close fighting. Keep your fist tight to your armpit, and with all your body weight, swing your elbow completely forward until it is pointing straight out in front of you. Intended targets include the ribs, solar plexus, throat, and jaw. By striking up, the elbow can be used to hit under the jaw, and by striking straight down, the point can be used to strike the base of the neck or the nose.

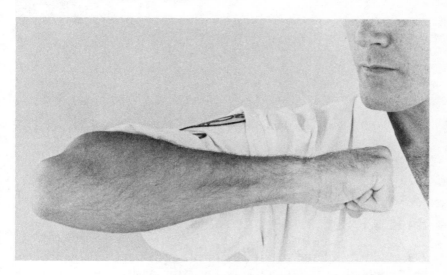

Four-Knuckle Fist

Bend the fingers halfway down keeping the thumb pulled in. This weapon is used exclusively for striking the throat and is called *hiraken*.

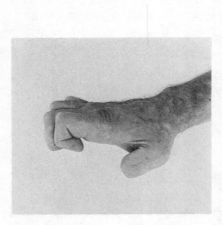 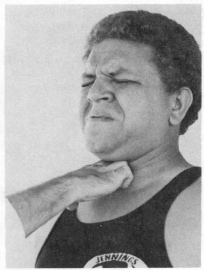

STRIKING

The majority of the previously mentioned hand techniques will be presented in Chapter 7. Along with basic kicks I feel the application of these techniques to a realistic self-defense situation will give the reader a better understanding of the purpose of each hand strike.

During training sessions, each hand technique should be executed full power for a minimum of 25 repetitions, while positioned in a strong front stance. They can be performed by being stationary or while moving up and down the *dojo* (training hall) floor. The forefist, palm heel, spear hand, claw hand, and four-knuckle fist are delivered from the hip on a direct line to the target, while the back fist, hammer fist, knife hand, ridge hand, and elbow strike are delivered from the hip in an arching

HOW TO STRIKE: FRONT VIEW. Above, left: Stand in a front stance with one arm extended to the solar plexus, while keeping the back hand flat on the hip, with the elbow tucked in toward the rib cage. Keep both fists in the vertical position (tate zuki). Above, right and below, left: Begin to pull the outstretched arm in as you strike to the solar plexus with the back hand. Below, right: The momentum created by this alternating motion increases your punching power. With one hand held back you are always ready to follow up with another strike if needed.

HOW TO STRIKE: SIDE VIEW. A side view of the basic straight punch illustrates the alternating motion your punches should have.

Whenever practicing your punching techniques, always train as though an attacker your size were standing directly in front of you. This will bring your strikes into the vital areas as this perfectly placed punch to the solar plexus shows.

motion to the target. When striking, the main points to remember are: Maintain a strong stance, keep the hips straight with the head up and back erect, and keep the body relaxed until the last moment of impact when air is expelled and all muscles are tightened. The basic principles behind all upper body karate strikes is exemplified by the following demonstration of the basic thrust punch to the solar plexus using the verticle fist *(tate zuki),* which is most commonly associated with the Isshin Ryu Karate system.

An incorrect punch: Instead of striking inward to the solar plexus, the strike is executed straight out from the hip completely missing the target. This can be corrected by practicing your punches in front of a mirror using your own image as a target.

DEVELOPING A STRONG GRIP

Possessing strong gripping power can be as important as a powerful strike. It is sad to say, but grip training is greatly neglected by many karate practitioners. A weak grip will never hold the knife-slashing hand of a crazed attacker. The following exercises are especially designed for improving hand strength. They should be practiced no less than two days per week.

1. fingertip pushups
2. knuckle pushups
3. hand squeeze
4. wrist curl

FINGERTIP PUSHUPS. Fingertip pushups are performed with your arms straight, balancing your weight high on the tips of your fingers, keeping the back, legs, and head straight. Then, lower your body to your wrists. Repeat for 50 repetitions.

KNUCKLE PUSHUPS. Knuckle pushups are performed by keeping the hands in a tightly formed fist. Concentrate all your body weight on the two large knuckles and begin in the up position. Then, bring your body down until it is even with your wrists. Repeat for 50 repetitions. Besides strengthening the hands and wrists, knuckle pushups also develop calluses for breaking.

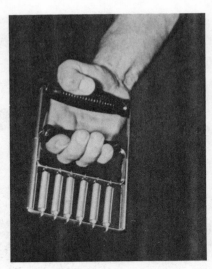 

HAND SQUEEZE. Hold the hand grip firmly, then squeeze it as hard as possible, trying to bring the two handles together. Perform 50 repetitions with each hand daily.

WRIST CURL. In a seated position, rest your forearms on your thighs with your hands out over your knees. Holding the bar, let your hands drop down, knuckles facing the floor. Curl the bar up as far as possible, squeezing it tightly. This exercise is number one for strengthening the forearm muscles which greatly affect hand strength. Do two sets of 25 repetitions.

WEIGHT TRAINING EXERCISES FOR GREATER UPPER BODY STRIKING POWER

1. bench press
2. lat pulldown
3. back rowing
4. shoulder press

5. shoulder flyers
6. arm curls
7. tricep pushdown
8. situps

BENCH PRESS. The bench press is a super exercise for adding greater thrusting power to your punches. Lying flat on a horizontal bench, lift the weight off the support rack and hold it in the up position, keeping your arms straight. Slowly lower the weight to your chest, then press it back up. Important breathing note: Inhale as the bar comes down. Exhale as you press it up. Do three sets of eight to ten repetitions.

LAT PULLDOWN. Lat machine pulldowns isolate and strengthen the *latissimus dorsi* muscles, which support the chest and arm when striking. Begin by gripping the bar as wide as possible, keeping the arms straight. Pull the bar down behind your neck until it touches, then slowly return it to the up position. Again, exhale as the bar comes down, inhale as you let it up. Do three sets of eight to ten repetitions.

BACK ROWING. Another great back exercise is bent over rowing, which should immediately follow lat pulldowns. Begin by standing over the weights with your feet shoulders' width apart, holding the bar with your elbows bent. Pull the bar up until the weights touch your chest. Be sure to concentrate on working only the back muscles. Breathing: Exhale as you pull the weight up, inhale as you let it down. Do three sets of eight to ten repetitions.

SHOULDER PRESS. The shoulder press (behind the neck) is number one for strengthening the shoulders, which are used most often when performing upper-body blocking techniques. In a seated position with your back placed firmly against a straight back bench, place the bar behind your neck resting it on the shoulders and gripping it beyond shoulders' width. Push the bar straight up behind you until the arms straighten. Lower the bar slowly, then repeat. Breathing: Exhale as you lift the bar, inhale as you lower it. Do three sets of eight to ten repetitions.

SHOULDER FLYES. Follow your shoulder presses with dumbbell flyes. Standing with your feet apart, lean forward 45 degrees, hold the dumbbells together at your waist, and keep your elbows bent. Complete the exercise by lifting your arms out to the sides until they are even with your shoulders, then return to the start position. Breathing: Exhale as you raise the dumbbells, inhale as they are lowered. Do three sets of 12 to 15 repetitions.

52

ARM CURLS. Bicep curls are used for greater bicep strength and development. Grip the bar at shoulders' width, holding it down near the thighs and keeping your elbows bent. Slowly curl the bar up until it is even with your shoulders. Hold it in the up position for three seconds, tightly squeezing your biceps before lowering the bar. Breathing: Exhale as you raise the bar, inhale as you lower it. Do three sets of eight to ten repetitions.

TRICEP PUSHDOWN. For total arm development, follow your curls with tricep pushdowns. Stand close to the bar, holding it at chin level with your hands approximately one foot apart. Push the bar down until your arms are straight. Slowly bring the bar up to the start position. Breathing: Exhale as you push down, inhale as you let the bar up. Do three sets of eight to ten repetitions.

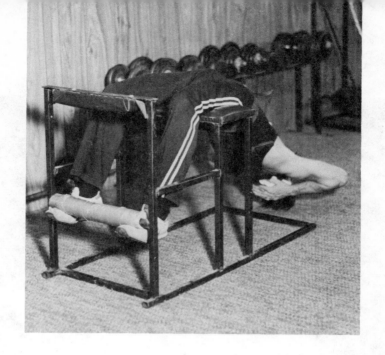

SITUPS. End your upper body weight routine with three sets of 25 situps. A rock-hard midsection is needed to withstand body strikes in self-defense or competition. When using a Roman chair, drop back with your head inches from the ground, keeping both hands behind the head. Then, pull yourself up to the seated position.

Photo by Madison Ford and Paul Slocum.

chapter five

devastating kicks

The one great advantage karate has over all other self-defense arts is the use of the legs. A karate kick has over five times the power of a punch, making it a truly awesome weapon to possess. Before you begin kicking, you must first master the six foot positions used when striking.

FOOT POSITIONS

Ball. Pull the toes back sharply and strike with the exposed padded area by keeping the foot straight on impact. The *koshi* or ball of the foot is used when executing front and roundhouse kicks.

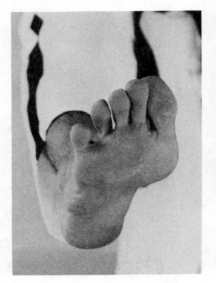 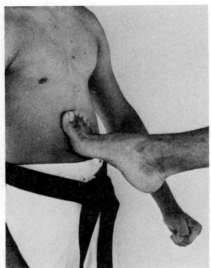

Blade. Accentuate the *sokuto* or outer edge of the foot by pulling the toes back and pushing the heel out. Used with side kicks to the ribs, solar plexus, throat, neck, or head.

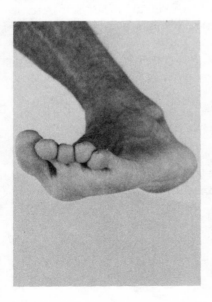 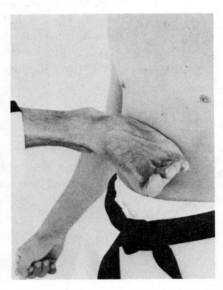

Heel. The *kakato* or heel is made by pulling the foot straight up and curling the toes back, as if trying to touch your toes to your shin. The heel should be used for all stomping techniques and back kicks.

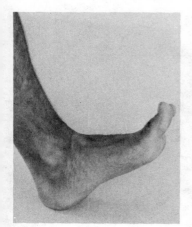

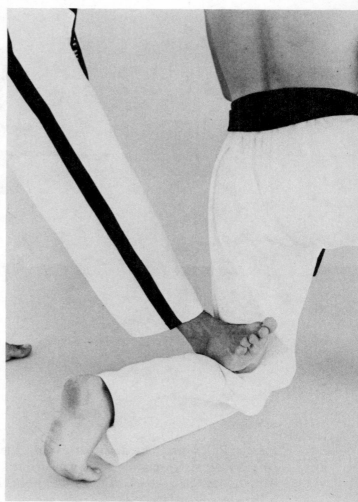

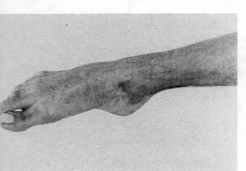

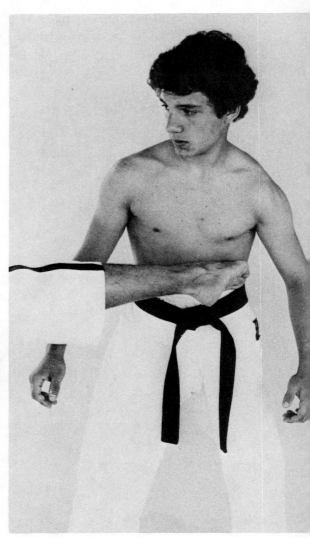

Instep. Pull your toes down to expose the top of the foot. The *haisoku* or instep can be used with front kicks to the groin and with roundhouse kicks to the ribs, groin, kidneys, solar plexus, neck, throat, or jaw.

Arch. The *achi* or arch area is made by pushing the heel out and pulling the toes back. The inside arch can be used to strike the knee, elbow, wrist, ribs, or side of the head.

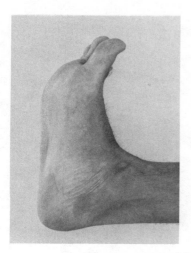

Knee. The top of the knee or *hiza* can be used for striking. Tuck the leg in and keep the toes pulled down so the foot is kept in the instep position. Knee strikes can be used to the groin, head, or midsection.

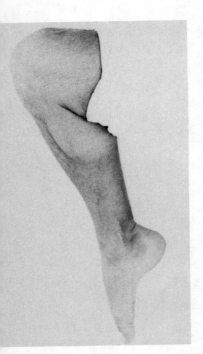

KICKING TECHNIQUES

Karate training consists of five different types of kicking techniques.

Snap kicks. Snap kicks are performed by striking out and immediately retracting the foot without hesitation. The snap kick is the most widely used in karate because the quick retraction protects the leg from being grabbed by your opponent. Since your balance is regained so quickly, snap kicks enable you to execute a series of kicks in quick succession with the same leg before setting it down. This type of multiple kicking is very popular among American tournament fighters.

Thrust kicks. Delivered the same way as the snap kick, but instead of retracting the kicking leg, the thrust kick is locked out for a full second. Thrust kicks act as an excellent defensive weapon when you wish to keep an opponent at a distance, such as a knife- or club-wielding attacker.

Wheel kicks. Wheel kicks are executed by swinging or whipping the leg at your opponent. Although wheel kicks are very powerful, they are used infrequently, being slower and more difficult to execute than snap or thrust kicks.

Stomping kicks. Used for very tight, in-close fighting situations, stomping kicks are delivered by driving the heel into the attacker's knee or foot. If the attacker is down, they also can be used to strike the groin, solar plexus, ribs, or head.

Flying kicks. Flying kicks are the most spectacular of all the karate kicks to observe. They were first developed to dismount riders from horses and to snap the necks of armour-plated warriors. Many hours of training are required to master flying kicks because of their high degree of difficulty. They are an excellent kick to use in free fighting competition and should be practiced regularly as a means of building leg strength and stamina.

Any kick can become a flying kick by simply becoming airborne, so try experimenting on the heavy bag at your gym with all your kicking techniques.

INCORRECT KNEE POSITION. Knee held too low, leaving the midsection vulnerable to an attack.

CORRECT KNEE POSITION. Knee held high into the chamber. Protects midsection and offers greater kicking mobility.

KICKS

Karate kicks are generally more difficult to master than hand techniques because of the loss of stability from balancing on one leg. Therefore, a great deal of time and effort must be put into perfecting them. The following basic and advanced kicks are karate's most effective. Basic kicks consist of the front, side, back, roundhouse, and stomp, while the advanced kicks are the hook, crescent, and flying kicks.

FRONT KICK. In a guard position, keeping your upper body straight . . .

. . . raise your rear leg high into the chamber. . . .

65

 . . . Snap out to solar plexus . . .   . . . and head.

SIDE KICK. Guard position. . . .

. . . Bring the front knee up high with the foot in a blade position. . . .

devastating kicks

. . . Strike the knee. . . .

. . . Turn the hip and supporting foot in the opposite direction as you kick strike the solar plexus. . . .

. . Strike head.

67

BACK KICK. Whenever kicking behind, always keep your eye on your opponent by looking over the kicking leg shoulder. . . .

. . . To get height with the back kick, tilt forward. . . .

. . . Strike solar plexus. . . . . . . Strike face.

**BACK LEG
ROUNDHOUSE KICK.
Ready position. . . .**

. . . Raise your rear leg, pointing your knee in the direction of your opponent. . . .

. . . Sharply turning your supporting foot and body, drive your kick at the head area. This also can be used for striking the groin, ribs, solar plexus, and kidneys.

FRONT LEG ROUNDHOUSE KICK. Not as strong as the back leg roundhouse, but faster. Slide your back leg up. . . .

. . . Bring the front leg high and turn your support foot and hips in the opposite direction as you snap your leg out, hitting with the instep. Targets include groin, solar plexus, ribs, throat, and face.

HOOK KICK. Ready position. . . .   . . . Slide up. . . .

. . . Shoot your leg out to the side of your opponent with the foot in a blade position. . . .

. . . Sharply hook your heel into   . . . and head area.
the midsection . . .

CRESCENT KICK. Perform the crescent kick by bringing the back leg up to your side. Then, swing your leg from the outside in with a circular motion across the front of your body. Keep the toes pulled back and make contact with the inside arch of the foot.

REVERSE CRESCENT KICK. Execute the reverse crescent kick by bringing your front leg slightly off the ground with your kicking leg hip pointed at your opponent. Then, swing your leg across the front of your body coming from the outside in. Keep the toes pulled back tightly to make contact with the outside edge, or blade, of the foot.

72

CROSSOVER HEEL STOMP. The crossover heel stomp is used for in-close encounters. Raise your stomping leg and drive your heel down and across into the side of your opponent's knee.

The flying kicks consist of the jump back leg roundhouse kick, jump spinning back kick, and the flying side kick.

KEY POINTS TO MASTERING KICKS

To master any of the karate kicks with maximum effectiveness the following principles must be applied:

1. Placement of the kicking knee before and after a kick's execution must be held high into the chest area. Bringing the knee up in this manner is commonly referred to as placing it *in the chamber,* or trigger position. A highly placed knee gives the kicker greater mobility, and helps protect the midsection against possible counterstrikes. When the knee is up, shift all your body weight on the supporting leg, keeping its knee slightly bent and the foot flat on the ground—even when kicking.

JUMP BACK LEG ROUNDHOUSE KICK. Jump high and at your opponent by bringing your rear leg to the front. In midair, turn your upper body sharply, executing a roundhouse kick by making contact with the instep.

A

2. After a kick has been thrown, immediately snap your kicking leg back to the chamber, holding it for the count of two before setting it down. This is an added precaution in case you miss your target and have to kick again without hesitation.

3. Since all kicks require the kicking foot to be held in a certain striking position to give the kick its maximum power, pay close attention to this in your training to avoid injuries. It makes no sense to disable your attacker with a kick and break your foot because it was improperly positioned.

4. Always be able to follow up your kicking techniques with blocks and punches. This is achieved by keeping your upper torso as erect as possible, and guard tight to your midsection.

5. For greater kicking power, keep the body relaxed until the last moment of contact when all the muscles must tighten. For a kick to score without detection, avoid giving it away by making jerking movements prior to its execution.

B

C

JUMP SPINNING BACK KICK. The jump spinning back kick is an excellent defensive fighting technique. As your opponent executes a back-leg roundhouse kick to your head, slap the kick away with an open palm block. . . .

. . . Immediately jump straight up in the air turning 180 degrees so your back is facing your opponent. . . .

. . . Looking over your kicking leg shoulder, execute a back kick to the face.

FLYING SIDE KICK. Execution of *Tobi Yoko Geri* (flying side kick) is done by running from five to ten steps, then jumping and turning the body sideways in midair. As you turn, thrust your lead leg out with the foot in the blade position. Keep the other leg tucked in tightly to protect the groin from a possible counterstrike. The lead hand should be extended out over the kicking leg to protect the ribs. The other hand should be held back near the rear hip in case a follow-up punch is needed.

WEIGHT TRAINING FOR MORE POWERFUL KICKS

The following three weight training exercises are all you will need for developing more powerful thrust and snap in your kicks. They should be performed two days a week immediately after completing your upper-body weight routine. As with the upper body, perform three sets of each exercise of no less than eight repetitions using a weight that will make you work hard to complete the last two reps. End your leg routine with squat jumps and ten minutes of light stretching.

THIGH EXTENSIONS. Thigh extensions work in strengthening the front thigh muscles and the knees. They will greatly increase the speed and snapping motion of your kicks. In a seated position, place your feet under the lift bar and tightly grip the sides of the bench with your hands. Slowly lift your legs up until they are parallel to the floor. At this point lock your knees out straight for three seconds before lowering. Breathing: Breathe rhythmically during repetitions. Do three sets of 12 to 15 repetitions.

REVERSE LEG CURLS. Reverse leg curls will strengthen the hamstring muscles located behind the thighs, helping to prevent injuries in this area during stretching and kicking exercises. Lying on your stomach, hold your legs out straight with your feet under the bar. Using a weight that will enable you to curl the bar up to your buttocks, slowly raise the weight. Breathing: Breathe rhythmically. Do three sets of 12 to 15 repetitions.

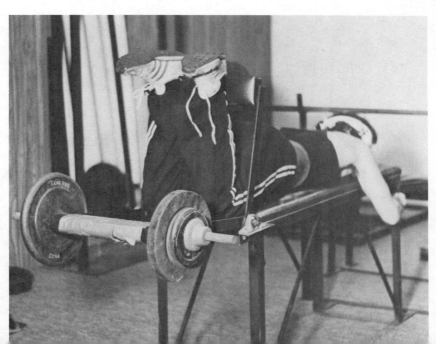

SQUATS. Squats are super for improving the thrusting power of your kicks and also will help you to achieve greater height in your flying kicks. With the aid of a squat rack, stand with your feet at shoulder's width apart, holding the weight on the back of your shoulders and keeping your upper body straight. Slowly squat down until your thighs are almost parallel to the floor. Breathing: Inhale on the way down, exhale when coming up. Do three sets of eight to ten repetitions.

80

SQUAT JUMPS. Top off your lower-body, weight-lifting routine with partner squat jumps. With your partner down on all fours, spring over him back and forth from one side to the other as quickly as possible for 50 repetitions.

chapter six
effective blocks

Possessing an effective defense is vital if one is to survive any type of assault. If you cannot stop your attacker's initial move with a well-placed block, you may never get a second chance. Karatekas spend many hours perfecting an arsenal of different blocking techniques which come under the heading of hard and soft. Hard blocks are powerful, straight-lined strikes that meet the attacker's strike full force, while soft blocks are openhand, circular movements that deflect the attacker's strike, often sending him off balance. Although they are equally effective, hard blocks are more popular because they are easier to master than the sometimes complicated movements of the circular blocks. Therefore, we will concentrate on mastering the hard blocks exclusively. It should also be noted that certain leg techniques such as the crescent kick and the knee also are used in blocking.

Besides being a defensive move, blocks can also work as an offensive weapon. A well-placed block to a major joint such as the knee, elbow, or ankle can disable an attacker as effectively as a punch or kick. My teacher, Master Angi Uezu, proved this once when he was attacked as he left a restaurant. As his attacker punched at his face, he stepped back and came across with an outside-inward, openhand block, which broke the attacker's wrist. As his attacker fell to the ground in great pain, there was no need for my teacher to follow up with a punch or kick. The block had ended the encounter.

To minimize injury when blocking with the arm, Isshin Ryu Karate stresses making contact with the forearm muscle and not the bone.

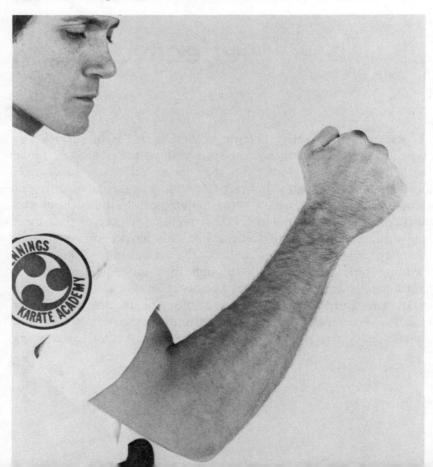

HARD BLOCKS

The following down, side, and head blocks are the most basic and commonly used defensive techniques in karate. Each of these direct line hard blocks can be executed by either keeping the fist closed or open. Open hand blocks are used to catch hold of and control your opponent's striking arm or leg. Included in this section is a forearm conditioning exercise for toughening the arms to withstand blows when blocking, and a resistance training exercise for building greater blocking strength.

KEY POINTS TO DEVELOPING STRONG BLOCKING TECHNIQUES

1. Start all blocking movements at one side of your body, always ending on the opposite side so you protect the entire area being blocked. Never block beyond the perimeter of your body. Overextended blocks will weaken your power and leave openings.

2. Put everything behind your blocks in the same way you would deliver a punch or kick.

3. Practice blocking techniques regularly. Have your training partner throw punches and kicks at you from all angles. Although it may be difficult to defend yourself at first, your reflexes will eventually improve to the point where it will be virtually impossible for your partner to break through your guard.

4. When executing a block, always be in a position to follow up with a strong punch or kick.

5. If the environment permits, always step back and away from your opponent when blocking to avoid getting hit full force if your block should miss its mark.

6. After the block has been completed, always retract the blocking arm to the hip.

7. For the split second a block is executed, lock together all your upper-body muscles to make the block immovable.

8. Practice your blocks equally with the right and left arms.

CLOSED FIST DOWN BLOCK. Start with both hands on the back leg hip side, placing the blocking hand on top. Sweep the block down across the body, keeping the elbow slightly bent. . . .

. . . Stop the block at the outside edge of your leg.

86

OPEN HAND DOWN BLOCK. Begin by blocking with the open palm of the hand to catch your opponent's kicking leg.

87

CLOSED FIST SIDE BLOCK. Sweep the block across the chest and midsection area by keeping the blocking arm elbow a fist away from your rib cage. . . .

. . . End the block with the outside edge of the forearm even with the outside edge of your shoulder.

OPEN HAND SIDE BLOCK. Sweep the block across the midsection making contact with the open outside edge of the hand. This block is used to grab hold and control your attacker's strike.

CLOSED FIST HEAD BLOCK. Starting position. Then sweep the block across the chest and face. Stopping just above the forehead, keep the arm bent and palm of the blocking hand facing down at your nose to accentuate the forearm muscle.

OPEN HAND HEAD BLOCK. Besides defending against a punch, the open hand head block is an excellent technique to use against an overhead knife or club attack. It enables the practitioner to hold and control the weapon hand.

CRESCENT KICK BLOCK. Swing your leg at your target, blocking with the arch of the foot.

KNEE BLOCK. Block by raising your knee to your elbow; it offers excellent protection against kicks to the midsection.

BLOCK CONDITIONING EXERCISES

The following photos illustrate exercises for forearm conditioning and resistance training for stronger blocks.

FOREARM CONDITIONING. This forearm conditioning exercise can be used for toughening the arms to withstand blows. When blocking, stand in a front stance, toe-to-toe with your partner with both hands on your hips in a blocking position. . . .

. . . Execute side and down blocks making hard contact with the forearm muscle.

RESISTANCE TRAINING FOR STRONGER BLOCKS. An excellent way to add strength to your blocking techniques is resistance training. Execute the side and head blocks by having your partner hold your blocking arm, making you strain to bring the block to its completed position. Do each block five times each.

93

chapter seven

environmental self-defense

It can easily be said that 99 percent of the American public have absolutely no idea how to defend themselves. This fact is very disturbing, considering the latest FBI reports which indicate that a physical crime is committed every 90 seconds in the United States. Everyone is a potential victim of an ugly mugging, rape, or murder, no matter where he or she may live or work.

This chapter will take the material specifically given in the previous chapters and apply it to the most common types of self-defense situations.

People trained in karate can enjoy the self-confidence of being able to defend themselves against any type of unarmed attack. Of course, no matter how skilled you are, the safest way to deal with any confrontation is to flee. However, this is not always possible. If backed into a corner, you have no choice but to do whatever is necessary to keep your attacker from harming you. At that point, no matter that your personality may usually be mild-mannered, it must change to that of a human fighting machine, ten times fiercer than your attacker, if you are to survive an assault. A skilled karateka in defense of his life or loved ones can be an attacker's worst nightmare.

If confronted with an unarmed attack, most people will generally do one of three things: (1) panic, and freeze at the mere sight of an assailant, enabling the attacker to do whatever he wants; (2) plead with an attacker in hopes of talking him out of causing harm; or (3) react by immediately disabling the attacker without hesitation or fear.

The last reaction listed is the only one you will want to take if unable to escape an unarmed attack. As the old saying goes, "He who hesitates is lost." In self-defense we say, "Those who hesitate are dead."

The way you will react can be judged by the way you train in karate. If you lazily train with little effort, you cannot expect to do much better in the street. But if you attack your workouts with great spirit and put out 100 percent, you can be sure to come out on top in a self-defense situation. Mastering the art of self-defense is not something that can be done in three easy lessons. It takes the guidance of a good teacher and a minimum of one year of formal karate training (almost the equivalent of achieving a green belt) to develop the proper balance, speed, power, and reflexes to become a formidable force.

ONE-ON-ONE, UNARMED SELF-DEFENSE

The following photos illustrate various forms of self-defense against a single attacker.

DOUBLE WRIST HOLD. With your opponent holding both wrists . . .

. . . raise your kicking leg. . . .

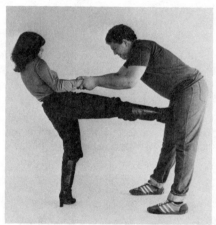

. . . Snap a front kick to the groin. . . .

. . . Retract the kick . . .

. . . and follow up with another front kick to the face.

FRONT BEAR HUG. Attacker appears and grabs you around the waist, leaving your hands free. Swing your hands out to the sides with your palms cupped. Smash palms to ears. Trigger knee and drive knee into groin.

SEATED ATTACK. Attacker appears . . .   . . . grabs shoulder. . . .

. . . Raise hammer fist. . . .

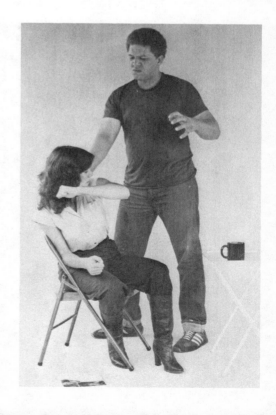

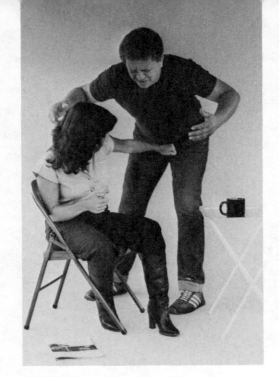

. . . Punch groin. . . .

. . . Follow up with elbow to face.

PURSE SNATCH. Attacker
appears from behind . . .

. . . grabs purse. . .

. . . As he pulls away, step
behind toward the at-
tacker . . .

. . . drive a blade kick into the side of the attacker's knee. . . .   . . . With other leg ready . . .

. . . follow up with a roundhouse kick to the bridge of the nose.

HEAD LOCK. Head lock position, your arms and legs are free. Reach for attacker's hair and prepare to stomp his knee from behind. . . .

. . . Pull attacker's hair back as you drive his knee to the pavement. . . .

. . . Follow up with a downward elbow strike to the bridge of the nose.

104

DOUBLE PUNCH ATTACK. Guard ready as attacker begins punch to head. . . .

. . . Block second punch to the midsection with same blocking arm. . . .

. . . Tight fist head block. . . .

. . . Again with same arm, pre-   . . . Back fist jaw. . . .
pare back fist. . . .

. . . Follow up with reverse punch to solar
plexus.

LAPEL GRAB. Attacker grabs lapel. . . .

. . . Grab attacker's hand and begin to push up on his elbow. . . .

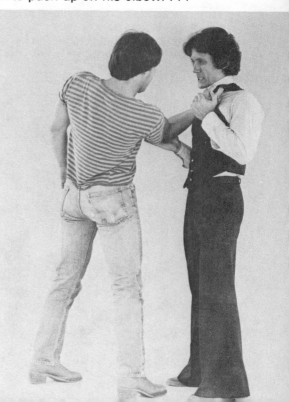

. . . Pull his hand down and push his elbow up, flipping attacker to the floor. Hold attacker to the floor. If he tries to move, apply more pressure; his shoulder joint will be in excruciating pain. At this point, I'm sure he will agree to leave you alone.

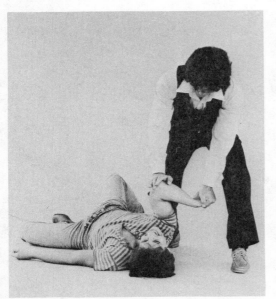 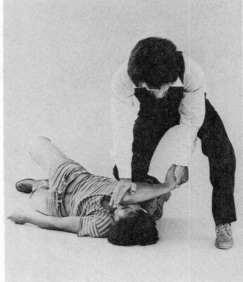

ONE-PUNCH ATTACK. Sensing your attacker's punch to the face, duck under his strike. Counter with a ridge hand to the solar plexus. . . .

Stepping behind your attacker, follow up with a claw hand strike to the throat, flipping him to the ground. . . .

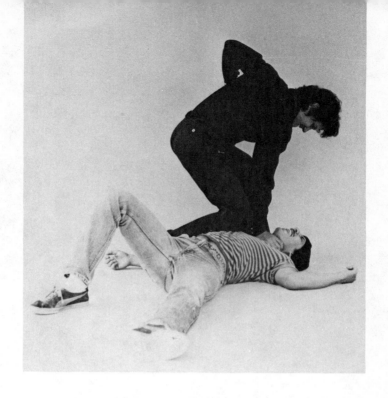

. . . Execute a straight punch to the nose.

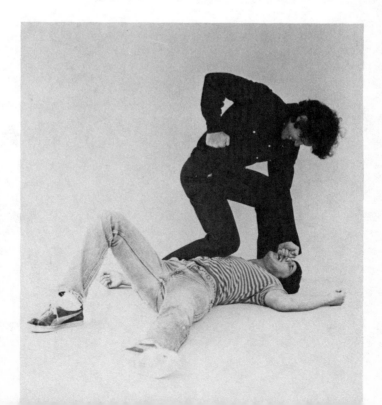

SIDE ATTACK. Attacker comes at you from the side, grabbing your shoulder. As he punches, raise your arm to block. . . .

Because he is still holding your shoulder, do not stop your block but continue it in a complete circle, tying up your attacker's arms in your armpit area. . . .

. . . At this point he will be unable to pull away from you. Follow up with a straight punch to the solar plexus and a blade kick to the back of the knee.

TWO-MAN ATTACKS

Without karate's great emphasis on the use of the legs, it would be virtually impossible to defend against two or more attackers. If one has hold of your arms, you can equalize the fight by dealing destructive kicks to his partner. The main point when dealing with two attackers is to always keep your eyes on both of them to avoid getting sucker-punched as one tries to distract you. Also try to disable one of them as quickly as possible. By immediately dropping one, you may create such a damaging psychological effect on his partner that he may not come near you. Assailants that work in groups are cowards, basically, and have little courage to "work" alone.

TWO-MAN FRONTAL ATTACK. With two attackers at 45-degree angles to your left and right, keep your eyes on both of them. . . .

. . . As one tries to come at you to grab hold, execute a front kick to his groin. . . .

. . . Set your kicking leg down, turning your opposite hip toward the second attacker. . . .

116

. . . As he comes in to punch you, execute a side thrust kick to his rib cage. . . .

. . . Follow up with a knee to his nose.

FULL NELSON CLUB ATTACK. Held from behind in a full nelson, cup your palms to your forehead and apply pressure so your attacker cannot bend your head forward. As the second attacker comes in to strike at your head with a club, jump up and kick him under the jaw. . . .

. . . After setting down, kick straight up into the other attacker's groin. . . .

. . . As he lets go, reach down, grab his ankle, and pull up, sending him to the ground. . . .

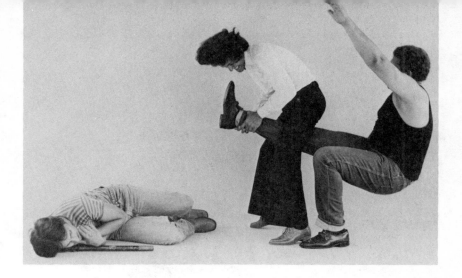

. . . Follow up with a heel stomp to the groin.

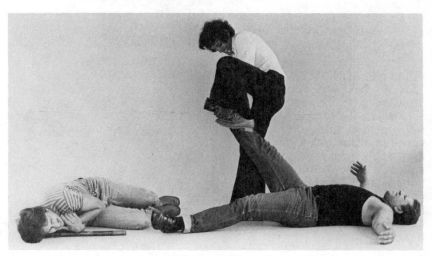

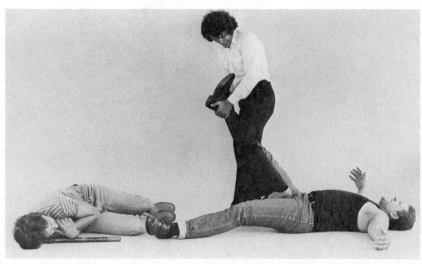

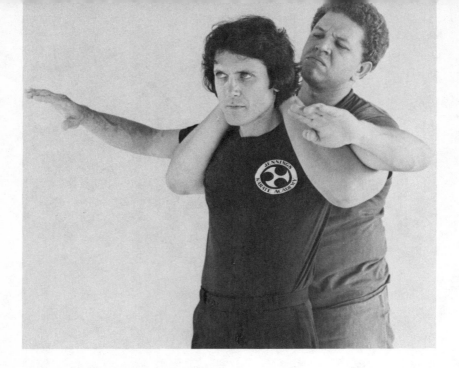

FULL NELSON RESIS-
TANCE. To keep your
attacker from bending
your head forward in a
full nelson hold, cup
your fingertips together
and apply pressure to
your forehead. Your op-
ponent will be unable
to move your head,
thus preventing your
neck from possibly be-
ing broken.

IMPORTANT POINTS TO REMEMBER IN AN UNARMED SELF-DEFENSE SITUATION

1. Never take your eyes off your attacker. If there is more than one, position yourself so you can observe each of them.

2. Never underestimate your attacker. Treat him as the world's deadliest person.

PRIMARY TARGETS

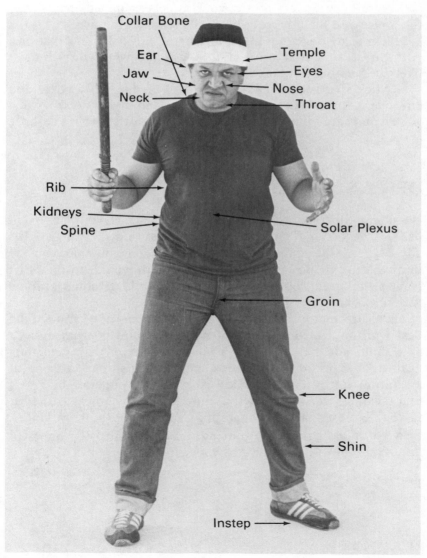

3. Never show fear no matter how you may feel inside. By itself, a strong, confident look can be capable of deterring an attack.

4. Once you have started your attack, follow through. *Do not hesitate.* Pick your targets and explode your technique into your attacker, holding back nothing.

5. If need be, grab whatever instruments lie nearby to assist you in your defense. For example, the use of a shovel or chair is excellent for warding off an assailant.

6. After you have stopped your attacker, immediately notify the police and file a report about exactly what happened.

7. Train by reacting to a variety of self-defense situations. Also, practice in your street clothes, which is what you will most likely be wearing if attacked.

8. Stick to basic techniques that will do the job quickly and effectively. In self-defense, avoid high and flying kicks which leave you more vulnerable than low kicks to the groin and knee areas.

DEFENSE AGAINST A WEAPON

No matter how skilled a fighter you may be, if your opponent has a weapon and you don't, you are at a disadvantage. His advantage is the ability to inflict injuries on you that you are incapable of giving in return. Just one stab wound to the heart from an innocent looking three-inch pocket knife could kill you within seconds.

There are many factors that will determine how you should deal with an armed attacker. If he has a blunt instrument such as a club, you have a better chance of victory than defending against a knife or gun. Unless an attacker's only reason for assaulting you is to harm or kill you, always cooperate by giving him whatever he wants when a knife or gun is shown. However, if you feel even after cooperating, your life is still in danger, then you must gamble by moving on your attacker in hopes of disabling him without injury to yourself.

There are techniques capable of dealing with the most dire situations. To increase the chances of their success, it is important to react to an armed attacker as follows: Keep relaxed for greater speed and at no time give your assailant the feeling you are going to try something. Build his confidence by pleading with him not to hurt you. Your initial technique must be to move the weapon from its lethal line of fire and to control the weapon hand. Once this is done, immediately follow with a disabling blow.

OVERHEAD CLUB ATTACK. Keep cool and wait for your attacker to begin his initial move. As he begins to raise the club, explode with a jump side kick to the solar plexus.

GUN AT HEAD. In a situation like this, you have no choice but to act. With blinding speed, shift your head away from the gun: at the same time, knock it up with your open hand and keep hold of the gun hand. Drive your knee into the attacker's groin and palm heel under his jaw.

126

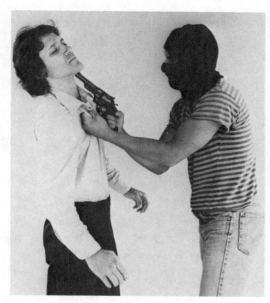

GUN AT THROAT. With your hands free, slap the gun away but keep hold of the gun hand. . . .

127

. . . Drive a blade kick to the
attacker's kneecap.

128

DEFENSE AGAINST A RIFLE.
Even though you are seated, you
can still react effectively. Shift
your head away from the line of
fire and slap the rifle behind you,
holding it. . . .

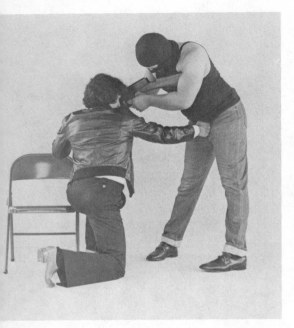

. . . Jump off the chair and punch the attacker in the groin, following up with an elbow to the jaw. . . .

. . . With your attacker weakened, hold the rifle securely and step behind, flipping him to the ground. If he still offers resistance, follow up with a rifle butt to the jaw.

 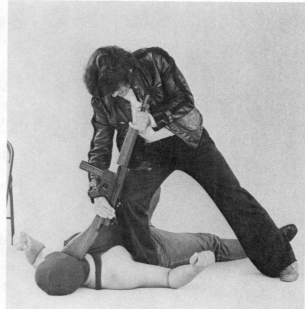

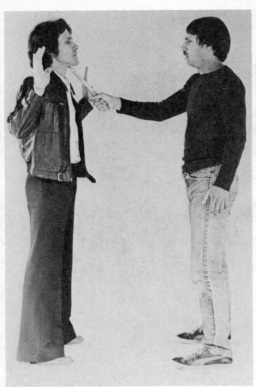

KNIFE AT THROAT. With the
hands held high, shift your
head away and slap the knife to
the side. Quickly grab and hold
the knife hand with your other
hand. . . .

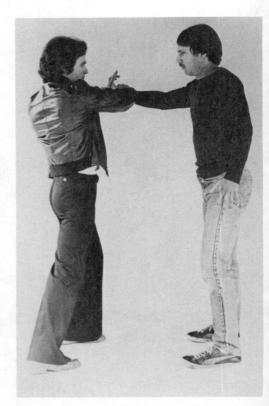

. . . Follow up with a four-knuckle strike to the throat.

133

chapter eight

sport karate: "american style"

At one point in your training, you are sure to experience the competitive aspect of karate, whether in the studio or at a tournament. Competition is very beneficial as a means of testing a student's skills and fighting spirit.

In the mid-'50s, a handful of American and Oriental promoters began presenting karate tournaments by modeling their events after Japanese competitions. The Japanese had an organized system of judging and scoring that enabled competitors to engage in sparring matches without injury. The man who devised this system was Tsutomu Ohshima, a student of Master Gichin Funakoshi, the founder of modern-day karate. Although there have been some changes and modifications of the rules and

135

procedures over the years, American promoters still use the Ohshima concept as the foundation for their events.

Early American tournaments were usually nothing more than a social gathering of local martial artists, consisting of few competitors. As the popularity of the martial arts began to sweep across America in the late '60s and early '70s, so did the popularity of karate tournaments. The once small gathering became a national event, with many tournaments drawing over 1,000 competitors eager to test their skills. In fact, in 1974, Ed Parker's International Karate Championships in Long Beach, California, drew 6,000 competitors, a record that stands today.

The fighting style of today's competitors differs greatly from that of past fighters. Fighters of the early '60s were much more traditional in their style. Although the fighters were very strong, their styles were rather predictable. They would fight from a deep horse stance, scoring the majority of their points with basic side kicks, front kicks, and reverse punches. Today's fighter is much more flashy and flamboyant in his movements and possesses a greater arsenal of attacks and counters, making American point competitors the world's best. Although techniques and fighting styles have changed, today's fighters are not necessarily superior to champions of the past. Early champions such as Chuck Norris, Joe Lewis, Bill Wallace, and Mike Stone could probably dominate the tournament scene of any era because of the hard-working qualities they possess.

Sport karate in America has been divided into two distinct categories: semicontact, or "point karate," and full-contact, or "knockout karate." Semicontact is a form in which competitors are required to control their kicks and punches, making only light contact without injuring their opponent. Full-contact karate is a form in which competitors fight in a roped ring and hold back nothing as they try to knock each other out with full-power kicks and punches to the head and midsection. (Because of its controlled techniques and wide appeal among competitors, the sparring techniques featured in this book are designed for the point karate player wishing to improve his or her skills.)

Although hundreds of point tournaments are held yearly, a few stand out as America's best. The reason for this is their proven track record for professionalism, fair judging, outstanding awards, national media coverage, and ability to attract top rated forms and fighting competitors from throughout the United States. I highly recommend that you attend one of these shows during your karate career. Witnessing America's top competitors in action can be inspirational and a great learning experience. The following tourneys are those that I consider to be among America's finest. All are promoted on a yearly basis.

1. The International Karate Championships (Long Beach, California)
2. The Battle of Atlanta (Atlanta, Georgia)
3. The United States Karate Association's Grand Nationals (location varies)

4. The Diamond Nationals (Minneapolis, Minnesota)
5. Fort Worth Pro-Am (Fort Worth, Texas)
6. American Karate Association Grand Nationals (Chicago, Illinois)

The exact dates of these events can be found in the calendar-of-events sections of major martial arts magazines such as *Black Belt, Karate Illustrated, Inside Kung-Fu, Kick,* and *Official Karate.* These are monthly publications and can be purchased at any newsstand. Besides presenting major events, they also list many smaller, regional tournaments you may wish to attend.

TOURNAMENT EXPENSES

If tournament competition appeals to you and you wish to pursue it on a regular basis, it is important that you start budgeting your money for upcoming events, which can prove to be very expensive. Most tournaments offer three categories of competition: kata (forms), weapons kata, and sparring. The average entry fee for each category is $12. If you plan on competing in all three events, you can easily see how expensive it can get. Besides your entry fee, you also have to consider other expenses—such as gas, food, and lodging—if it is an overnight trip. To help ease the cost, it is wise to travel in a group of four or more to split expenses and to hold school fundraising activities, such as car washes, paper drives, and raffles. Through such activities, twelve of my students were able to raise $2,000 toward a trip to Georgia for the 1980 *Battle of Atlanta.*

DIVISIONS

Karate tournaments offer divisions to accommodate men, women, and children of every belt rank and most weight divisions. Below is a list of divisions taken directly from the 1981 *Battle of Atlanta,* one of America's leading karate tournaments since 1969. Study them carefully to decide which division pertains to you.

Divisions

KIDS 5-7 ALL BELTS FIGHTING
KIDS 8-10 WHITE & GREEN: FIGHTING
KIDS 11-13 WHITE & GREEN: FIGHTING
KIDS 14-15 WHITE & GREEN: FIGHTING

KIDS 8-10 BROWN AND BLACK: FIGHTING
KIDS 11-13 BROWN & BLACK: FIGHTING
KIDS 14-15 BROWN & BLACK: FIGHTING

KIDS 5-10 FORMS (WHITE & GREEN)
KIDS 5-10 FORMS (BROWN & BLACK)

KIDS 11-15 FORMS (WHITE & GREEN)
KIDS 11-15 FORMS (BROWN & BLACK)

IN MEN'S WHITE, GREEN AND BROWN BELT DIVISIONS: LT. WT. IS BELOW 150 lbs.
MID.WT. IS 150-170 lbs.
HVY. WT. IS OVER 170 lbs.

WOMEN: LT. WT. 120 AND BELOW: HEAVY OVER 120

WHITE BELT LT. FIGHTING: MEN
WHITE BELT MID. WT. FIGHTING: MEN
WHITE BELT HVY. FIGHTING: MEN
WHITE BELT FORMS: MEN

WHITE BELT LT. FIGHTING: WOMEN
WHITE BELT HVY. FIGHTING: WOMEN
WHITE BELT FORMS: WOMEN

GREEN BELT LT. FIGHTING: MEN
GREEN BELT MID. WT. FIGHTING: MEN
GREEN BELT HVY. FIGHTING: MEN
GREEN BELT FORMS: MEN

GREEN BELT LT. FIGHTING: WOMEN
GREEN BELT HVY. FIGHTING: WOMEN
GREEN BELT FORMS: WOMEN

BROWN/RED BELT LT. FIGHTING: MEN
BROWN/RED BELT MID. WT. FIGHTING: MEN
BROWN/RED BELT HVY. FIGHTING: MEN
BROWN/RED FORMS: MEN
BROWN/RED LT. FIGHTING: WOMEN
BROWN/RED BELT HVY. FIGHTING: WOMEN
BROWN/RED FORMS: WOMEN
UNDER BLACK BELT WEAPONS (MEN & WOMEN TOGETHER)

MEN BLACK BELTS SUP. LT. (130 & BELOW) FIGHTING
MEN BLACK BELTS LT. WT. (140-151) FIGHTING
MEN BLACK BELTS MD. WT. (152-165) FIGHTING
MEN BLACK BELTS LT. HVY (166-182) FIGHTING
MEN BLACK BELTS HVY. WT. (183 & ABOVE) FIGHTING

BLACK BELTS LT. WT. (120 & BELOW) FIGHTING WOMEN
BLACK BELTS HVY. WT. (OVER 120) FIGHTING WOMEN
BLACK BELT WEAPONS (MEN & WOMEN COMBINED)

1ST - 4TH IN THESE DIVISIONS
BLACK BELT: CHINESE FORMS
BLACK BELT: AMERICAN OPEN FORMS
BLACK BELT: WOMEN'S FORMS

BLACK BELT: JAPANESE FORMS
BLACK BELT: KOREAN FORMS
BLACK BELT: OKINAWAN FORMS

IMPORTANT POINTS TO REMEMBER
WHEN ATTENDING A TOURNAMENT

1. In advance of an upcoming event, familiarize yourself with the tournament by carefully going over the information sent out by the promoter concerning rules and procedures.

2. Before leaving, double-check to make sure you have all the proper gear. Since it is an all-day affair held on a weekend, it's wise to pack a big lunch.

3. Arrive early to register. After you have paid the required fees, get dressed and begin lightly warming up until your ring is called.

4. When your ring is called, quickly go to it and give the coordinator your name. Do not leave your ring after competing. All contestants will be dismissed as a group.

5. When everyone in your ring has competed, the winners will be announced. Trophies usually are awarded to all first, second, and third place winners, although some tournaments offer awards all the way up to eighth place. Some of the larger events also include cash awards as high as $1,000.

chapter nine

competitive sparring equipment

In the early days of American point tournaments, sparring competitors wore only a groin protector and mouthpiece as means of protection against injury. Most of those doing battle felt that to be sufficient because of the light contact rules that prevailed. Although early rules stressed no excessive contact, this was not always the case. Injuries occurred because of the lack of control by many competitors when executing a punch or kick to the point area of an opponent. These injuries occurred not so much from making light contact, but more from the bare hand and foot which could easily cut an opponent with the slightest amount of impact. This bare knuckle era is referred to as the "blood and guts" period of American karate competition. Instructors and tournament promoters began to realize that a covering for bare hands and feet was needed to eliminate the injury problem and make the matches less cautious and more exciting.

One man who felt he had the answer was Mr. Jhoon Rhee, a highly respected promoter and successful school operator from Washington, D.C. Mr. Rhee revolutionized American sport karate in 1973 with his invention of Safe-T-Punch and Safe-T-Kick training equipment. He developed lightweight hand and foot pads made of foam rubber that could be worn in competition to prevent injuries without restricting a competitor's performance. Enthusiastically received by the karate community, various brands of protective equipment are now used all over the world and are mandatory in 75 percent of open American tournaments.

EQUIPMENT

It is highly recommended that you purchase the following equipment within the first three months of your training. Besides its use in tournament competition, you will want to use it in your regular training program to prevent injuries. If your instructor or school does not stock the following items, you can

The proper protective equipment greatly minimizes the chance of injury to fighters and their opponents in semi-contact sparring competition.

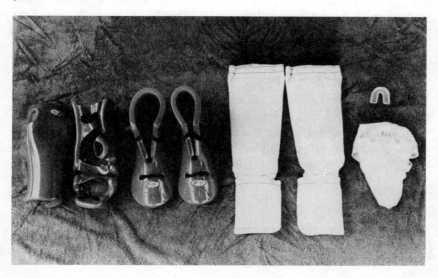

purchase them through mail order ads featured in most martial arts magazines. By taking care of your gear properly, it should last a lifetime.

Uniform. The karate *Gi,* as it is called in Japanese, comes in a variety of colors although white is still the most popular. For sparring competition, your suit should be of 100 percent light-weight cotton. Cotton has all the other materials beat for absorbing sweat and keeping you cool during a meet. Always look sharp by keeping your uniform clean and ironed.

Mouthpiece. A mouthpiece is a small but very important item. Made of rubber, it is placed in the mouth and held firmly in place by biting down. It keeps the jaw secure and teeth from striking each other, which could cause them to chip or break. Wear it at all times, whether training in the school or competing.

Groin protector. The "cup," as the groin protector is commonly referred to, is for male competitors only. Worn under the underwear, it is a fiberglass cup that covers and protects the testicles from injury. It is held in place by an elastic strap.

Shin and instep protector. A foam rubber pad, covered with canvas, which should be worn under the pant leg to protect the shin and instep from bruises that may occur when executing kicks.

Protective boot. A lightweight, foam rubber boot that protects the toes, instep, and ankle from injuries when kicking. It is secured to the bare foot with shoelaces.

Protective gloves. Foam-padded gloves worn to protect the fingers, knuckles, and wrists from injury. They also protect your opponent from being cut by a bare knuckle if contact is made to the face area. Although it completely covers the fist, its unique open palm design enables the wearer to grab hold of his opponent when executing a takedown or a grabbing technique.

chapter ten

judging—pros and cons

One of the biggest problems facing point karate competition in America today is the inconsistency of its judging. This stems from the fact that there is no governing body for karate in the United States. Unlike baseball or boxing, which have universal rules, karate has no national rules. The sport consists of numerous associations each having its own set of rules and procedures as well as the desire to remain fiercely independent. This lack of national unity has virtually created a free-for-all as to how each promoter chooses to have his sparring matches judged. The differences in rules from tournament to tournament can range from minor to extreme. For example, an event held in Ohio may allow competitors to perform takedown techniques, while a tournament on the West Coast won't even recognize such techniques. These discrepancies exist, and as a competitor you will have to be able to adjust to any rule changes that may occur during your competitive career.

Regardless of these differences, I find that the majority of American open tournaments adhere most closely to the following free fighting competition rules and procedures, which will serve as a general guide by which you can train. They pertain to all belt divisions.

1. *Fighting area.* All competitors will spar in a 20′ × 20′ ropeless ring.

2. *Equipment.* Formal uniform, mouthguard, groin protector, protective boot, protective glove, and shin and instep protector. Jewelry of any type may not be worn during competition.

3. *Officials.* Each ring will have five black belt judges, one in each corner and one in the center. The center referee controls the ring, having the responsibility of starting and stopping matches and awarding points. Each corner judge's job is to call points immediately as they are seen. Three out of five officials must agree on the same technique for a point to be awarded. A ring is not allowed to have more than one official from the same school judging.

4. *Match times.* Bouts will run for two minutes or the scoring of three points, whichever comes first. After two minutes, the competitor with the most accumulated points will be declared the winner. If no points have been scored after two minutes, the match will go into sudden death overtime. The first person to score a point will be declared the winner. (The same holds true for a tie after two minutes.)

5. *Scoring points.* All legal techniques scored will equal one point. Point areas include the head, chest, neck, stomach, rib cage, or kidneys. No points will be awarded to techniques aimed at the top of the head, spine, throat, groin, or knees. For a punch or kick to be called a point, it must be delivered with good balance, speed, power, focus, accuracy, and control. The contestant is allowed to make light face and body contact without injury to his opponent, although a point can still be called even without touching one's opponent as long as it is within one inch of the intended target.

6. *Excessive contact.* If a contestant strikes his opponent with lack of control causing broken bones, bruises, or blood, he will be warned or disqualified depending on the severity of the strike delivered and the decision of the five judges. If the judges decide

to give the contestant a warning, they will then award the person struck a full point. If a second infraction occurs during the match, the guilty contestant will be immediately disqualified.

7. *Running out of bounds.* A contestant is not allowed to evade his opponent by running out of bounds to stop the match. A contestant who does so will be warned once by the official, and if the infraction is committed a second time, his or her opponent will be awarded a point. Running out of bounds a third time will mean immediate disqualification.

8. *Conduct.* Any unsportsmanlike conduct—such as throwing equipment, cursing, ignoring instructions, or showing disrespect for an official or fellow competitor—is immediate grounds for disqualification.

9. *Holding.* A contestant is allowed to catch hold of his opponent's leg or sleeve as long as he immediately follows with a punch or kick. It is illegal to catch hold of your opponent and swing him wildly.

10. *Coaching.* Sideline coaching by instructors or fellow students is not allowed.

11. *Related competitors.* Students from the same school will be separated in the first round only.

12. *Bye system.* The purpose of the bye system is to even out the number of contestants in the first round. This will avoid any unfair advantages that may arise in the semifinals or finals. A count of the number of contestants in each sparring ring will be made and deducted from the next highest number on the following series of numbers: 4-8-16-32-64-128. The difference of these numbers will account for the number of byes that must be selected. If the number of contestants matches a number on the table, the bye system is not necessary.

Opponent on left scores with a perfectly placed backfist to the face.

149

chapter eleven

training to win offensive and defensive points

Before students engage in free fighting, they should be able to execute basic techniques with control and accuracy. Injuries often occur when an impatient student attempts to spar before he has mastered the fundamentals. Sparring may look easy from the sidelines but—like the performance of a fine kata—it takes months and even years to perfect.

Before you begin sparring, it is important to analyze your strong and weak points with the help of an experienced coach. For example, if you lack the necessary height and flexibility to execute advanced kicking techniques, you should avoid these and concentrate more on developing your hands in combination with a few basic kicks. I've seen fighters with great potential go nowhere because they trained in techniques unsuited to their physical makeup. Once you have established what your strong and weak points are, develop your own fighting style accordingly.

The object of point fighting is to tag your opponent with a controlled technique, rather than beating him into submission with brute strength. Therefore, you must develop an intelligent approach to tournament fighting. Like a game of chess, point fighting requires a good strategy to win.

RING STRATEGY

I have witnessed smaller fighters take apart their larger opponents because of good strategy. Although the stronger opponent may win in a street fight, this has little meaning in point competition. Winning ring strategy can be achieved by applying the following points:

1. When your match has been given the signal to begin, don't be in a hurry to attack your opponent. Take time to see what type of fighter he is by faking him to test his reaction. After a feint he will do one of three things: retreat, charge, or stay in one spot ready to block and counter your attack. This feinting tactic will give you a good idea of what techniques will be needed to score on him.

2. Constantly be alert to any weaknesses or openings your opponent may have. For example, if he fights from a very low, wide stance, he may be open to foot-sweeping techniques.

3. After you have determined your opponent's strong or weak points and the type of fighter he is, try to score the first point. Being in the lead, your opponent has no choice but to come to you. You can now set him up for a defensive counter which will bring you your second point.

4. Do not be influenced or intimidated by your opponent. Always stay in full control by fighting your own fight. If your opponent bounces around the ring in a rapid pace and you prefer to move more cautiously, it will do no good for you to

start bouncing like your opponent. It will destroy your timing and execution of technique.

5. Bait your opponent by leaving deceptive openings and setting him up for counter techniques.

6. Never attack when your opponent is in his strongest guard and stance. Breaking his concentration can be achieved by executing feints before an attack.

7. Be alert as to the distance between you and your opponent. If you can fully extend your arm and touch your opponent with your hand he is in a punching zone. If you cannot touch him, he is in a kicking zone. Always position your opponent into the zone you want him to be, without his being aware of it.

8. Never leave your fighting ring. Always stay on the sidelines to observe the fighters competing before and after your match because you will more than likely have to face one of them on your road to first place. Knowing their complete fighting style before bowing in for your match can prove to be a great advantage.

9. Get in the habit of executing a loud *kiai* when scoring a point to help draw the judges' attention to your technique.

Even when not competing, stay by your ring to observe other fighters you may end up facing later in the day.

Executing a loud kiai when landing a point in competition helps draw the judges' attention to your technique.

GETTING TO THE TOP

In my opinion, the American karate tournament scene is the toughest in the world. Where most countries present only a handful of competitions a year, there are numerous events held on a monthly basis throughout the United States. This gives American fighters a great opportunity to consistently test their skills and gain important experience. With such a vast amount of hard-hitting talent, you will have your work cut out for you if you plan on becoming the next United States' champion. Through much dedication and hard work, however, it is certainly not an impossible goal to achieve.

There are certain factors you will have to consider in your quest to reach the top. First of all, national recognition and titles are only given to black belt competitors. As a fighter, you will have to prove yourself by competing regularly in regional and national events that attract high-rated fighters. By winning consistently in these tournaments, you will begin to accumulate the points needed to put you at the top. In America, the rating systems are set up by karate magazines, who publish current tournament results on a monthly basis. Because rating systems are updated periodically, you should consult these magazines regularly for any changes that may affect you as a competitor.

154

OFFENSIVE POINTS

Very seldom in a sparring match will you be able to score a point by executing just one technique. A single technique can easily be blocked and countered by an experienced fighter. In point fighting, it is usually the second, third, and even the fourth technique that finds its mark. This is why the mastery of offensive combinations is vital if you hope to win consistently. Combinations work by confusing and taking apart your opponent's defenses. A flurry of combined techniques also greatly increases your chances of scoring a point.

It is good practice to learn many different combinations but wise to work on perfecting only a few. In a match, there isn't enough time to execute a hundred different kinds of attacks. Ideally, you should possess three offensive combinations you can score with at will. Ex-world middleweight karate champion Bill Wallace won almost all his preliminary and title fights with a side kick to the ribs, followed by a roundhouse to the head—a combination performed with the same leg. Although Wallace's opponents knew he would execute his trademark combinations during a match, they still were unable to defend against it. Wallace delivered it with such perfect timing and blinding speed that it was virtually impossible to stop. The point is, Wallace easily could have executed a number of techniques and combinations but he always stayed with the one he knew he had no trouble scoring with.

Besides all the other factors that go into the development of good sparring techniques, distancing is probably the most important factor when working combinations. In training, make sure every technique in the combination is capable of making contact with your opponent. This is achieved by compensating for your opponent's moving forward or backward during an encounter. Another thing to remember is that your first move is crucial in setting up your combinations. It must knock your man off balance and weaken his defense. Deliver it with the element of surprise and great force.

WINNING COMBINATIONS

The following offensive combinations have repeatedly put my students in the winner's circle. Work them to a degree of perfection, then feel free to incorporate any techniques you may favor in your training.

FAKE KICK—JUMP IN BACKFIST. Ready position. . . .

. . . Fake a kick with your lead leg and as your opponent takes the fake, jump in . . .

. . . scoring with a backfist to the head.

FAKE HEAD PUNCH—JUMP IN SIDE KICK. Ready position. . . .

. . . Slide in with a fake backfist to the head. . . .

. . . As your opponent raises his guard to block, jump in with a side kick to the midsection.

157

**FAKE LOW KICK—
ROUNDHOUSE TO
HEAD—SIDE KICK TO
MIDSECTION (ALL
WITH THE SAME LEG).**
Ready position. . . .

. . . Fake a low kick to
your opponent's groin
to upset his guard. . . .

. . . Bring the leg into
the kicking cham-
ber. . . .

158

. . . Follow with a roundhouse to the head, and end with a side kick to the ribs.

159

**FOOT SWEEP—JUMP
ROUNDHOUSE—PUNCH.
Ready position. . . .**

. . . With your back leg,
sweep your opponent's leg
with your instep. . . .

. . . With his balance shaken, immediately jump in the air and execute a roundhouse kick to the head with your back leg. . . .

. . . If your sweep has knocked your opponent to the ground, follow up with a reverse punch to the midsection.

ROUNDHOUSE—BACKFIST—STRAIGHT PUNCH. Ready position. Slide into your opponent, readying your lead leg for a front leg . . .

. . . roundhouse to the
midsection. . . .

. . . Then, set down into your opponent with a backfist to the head
and a reverse punch to the ribs.

**HOOK KICK—
ROUNDHOUSE
KICK—RIDGE HAND.
Ready position. . . .**

**. . . Slide up and bring
the front leg knee
up. . . .**

164

. . . Execute a hook kick to head . . .

. . . Without setting the kicking leg down . . .

. . . follow with a round-house to the face and . . .

. . . ridge hand to the temple.

FAKE PUNCH—FRONT KICK—SPINNING BACK KICK—REVERSE PUNCH. Ready position. . . .

. . . Fake a reverse punch to the head. . . .

. . . Follow with a front kick to the midsection . . .

. . . setting your kicking leg
down. . . .

. . . Execute a spinning
back kick to the face . . .

. . . setting around to face your opponent. End with a reverse punch to the solar plexus.

DEFENSIVE POINTS

As in self-defense where a good defense can mean the difference between life or death, in sparring competition it can mean the difference between victory or defeat. Since American fighters are generally very aggressive, the development of an effective defense plays an important part in establishing your fight strategy. In fact, some current champions are regarded as defensive fighters because of their ability to win most of their bouts by picking off their opponents with defensive techniques.

The biggest problem students have in developing a strong defense is the ability to hold their ground. This is understand-

SIDE KICK COUNTER. Sensing your opponent's punching attack, shift your body weight on the back leg and ready the front leg to counter. Counter a jump backfist with a perfectly timed side kick to the ribs.

170

able because the natural reaction to any attack is to move back. To help overcome this, train by standing with your back against a wall. Then have your training partner attack you with a variety of offensive sparring techniques. By working in this way, you will greatly improve your blocks and counters, giving you the confidence to hold your ground against the most aggressive opponents.

There are two types of defensive maneuvers. One is to counter your opponent by catching him in the midst of his attack, and the other is to evade your opponent's assault, catching him off balance as he is about to complete his offensive technique.

DEFENSIVE FRONT KICK. Ready position. . . .

. . . As your opponent begins a kicking attack, hold your ground and skip in while he is in midkick, executing a front kick with your lead leg to his midsection.

LEAN AWAY—COUNTER WITH PUNCH. Ready position. As your opponent kicks high to the head, keep your feet planted and lean away, out of reach of the kick. . . .

. . . Catch him with a reverse punch to the midsection as he sets the kicking leg down.

DEFENSE AGAINST FOOT SWEEP. Ready position. As your opponent's foot sweeps you . . .

. . . keep your motion going, setting the swept leg around and positioning yourself into a back kick position. Execute the back kick as your opponent attempts to follow his sweep with a punch.

BLOCK ROUNDHOUSE KICK—REVERSE PUNCH—RIDGE HAND COUNTER KICK. Ready position. As your opponent attempts a back leg roundhouse kick . . .

. . . raise your lead knee up to your elbow to protect your midsection. After the block, follow with a backfist to the head and a reverse punch to the solar plexus.

SWEEP KICK AWAY—COUNTER WITH PUNCH. Ready position. As your opponent delivers a roundhouse at your midsection . . .

. . . lean out of the way of the kick, slapping it to the side. . . .

. . . With your opponent off balance, follow up with a reverse punch to the kidneys and a ridge hand to the jaw.

179

BLOCK KICK—SPINNING BACKFIST COUNTER. Ready position. . . .

. . . Block your opponent's round-house kick by tightly crossing your arms, keeping one held high and one low. . . .

. . . Spin around and back into your opponent, following up with a backfist to your opponent's jaw.

TAKEDOWNS

By sending your opponent to the ground during a match, you can greatly weaken his confidence and upset his fighting rhythm. Takedowns will make your opponent feel vulnerable, which is all in your favor. To avoid injury to your opponent, takedowns must be executed with utmost caution on your part. Contact is made to your opponent just above the ankle and not directly to the knee or ankle joint. The following offensive and defensive takedowns will add to your defensive fighting strategy.

STEP BEHIND FOOT SWEEP—PUNCH. Ready position. Facing your opponent (opposite sides facing), slide in and fake a backfist to your opponent's head. Having upset his balance, grab his shoulder with your punching hand and step behind his lead leg. . . .

. . . As you pull him down, kick his leg out from under him. Follow with a punch to the head for a point.

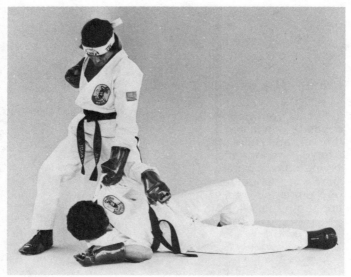

**CATCH ROUND-
HOUSE KICK—
TAKEDOWN.
Ready posi-
tion. . . .**

. . . As you block your opponent's back leg roundhouse kick, catch his leg and shoulder and hook your lead leg behind his supporting leg. Knock his supporting leg out from under him, bringing him to the ground. . . .

. . . Follow up with a reverse punch to the midsection.

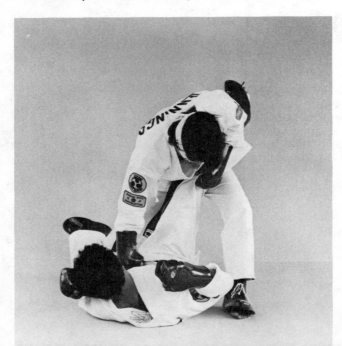

DROP SWEEP—PUNCH.
Ready position. . . .

. . . As your opponent attempts a front leg round-house kick to the head, drop under the kick . . .

. . . and swing your top leg around to catch your opponent above the ankle, sweeping him to the ground. . . .

. . . Follow up with a punch to the face.

FREE FIGHTING WORKOUT ROUTINE

To capture first place in semicontact competition you may have to fight anywhere from three to ten matches in one day, depending on the number of competitors in your division. The mental and physical strain of so many encounters can be endured only by being in top physical condition.

The following five-day-a-week workout is designed especially for the serious karate student wishing to improve his or her stamina and tournament skills. Do the following routine in the exact order shown, with as little rest as possible between exercises.

Monday, Wednesday, Friday

1. Stretch ten minutes.
2. Run two miles.
3. 75 squat jumps.
4. 150 situps.
5. 100 pushups. Do four sets of 25, with a 30 second rest in between sets.
6. Working in front of a mirror, execute 50 front kicks (25 each leg), 50 side kicks (25 each leg), and 50 front leg roundhouse kicks (25 each leg). Execute all kicks with the front leg skipping in as if charging your opponent. Each kick should be thrown at full power, alternating each from midsection to head height. Do not kick fast and sloppy. Move in front of the mirror as if sparring, always maintaining perfect form.
7. Shadow spar for two three-minute rounds by executing a variety of offensive and defensive sparring combinations, using the hands and feet. Concentrate on executing each technique with blinding speed. (Rest one minute between rounds.)
8. For one three-minute round, shadow spar by executing only your favorite offensive and defensive sparring techniques.
9. After resting for five minutes, perform two three-minute rounds on the heavy bag with a minute rest between rounds. When working the bag, pace yourself by fighting it like an

opponent. Move around the bag hitting it with combinations from different angles.

10. With a partner, spar hard for six to twelve minutes without stopping. Avoid acknowledging any points. The object of the exercise is to work your techniques hard.

11. End with ten minutes of light stretching exercises.

Tuesday and Thursday

1–6. Repeat the *Monday, Wednesday, Friday* warmups.

7. With a partner holding two hand mitts and moving about the floor simulating your opponent, execute your most favored offensive and defensive techniques for ten consecutive minutes.

8. With the help of fellow students and instructors, recreate four three-minute sparring matches as closely as possible to the way they are run at tournaments you attend in your area, judges and all. After each match, win or lose, discuss the strong and weak points of your fights. Feedback from students and instructors will give you great insight into how to improve your fight strategy. Take criticism as constructive and beneficial, not as a putdown.

Frequent tournament competition gives the karateka added experience and confidence to master winning techniques.

Attending fighting seminars by champions like Bill Wallace are sure to give you greater insight into ways of perfecting your sparring techniques.

INSIDE SPARRING TIPS

1. Compete in as many tournaments as possible to gain experience and to observe the winning techniques of other fighters.

2. Stop all training two days prior to a tournament so the body will be well-rested for the upcoming event. Use the rest period as a time to psych yourself up mentally.

3. A good fighter is a well-rounded fighter. Concentrate on developing offensive and defensive techniques equally. Favoring one over the other will weaken your fight game.

4. Because you are sure to face opponents of different *sizes* in tournaments, train by fighting a variety of people with different *belt ranks* at your studio.

5. In training, reenact tournament matches by running them the exact way they are presented at events you are attending. This will aquaint you with the rules and help eliminate nervousness.

6. Many promoters feature sparring clinics by top-rated fighters prior to their tournaments. You should make it a point to attend these clinics as often as possible. The winning techniques and strategies of the champs can give you great insight into ways of improving your fight game.

7. After any match, win or lose, analyze the way you fought. Work on correcting any mistakes made.

8. Train religiously. If you miss a workout, be sure to make it up. The day you goof off is the day your opponent trained.

9. At all times, keep a positive mental attitude. Believe you can win and you will.

189

chapter twelve

winning kata

Kata is a series of prearranged movements signifying an imaginary fight against several opponents. The special techniques incorporated into the katas were first developed by early masters who actually used many of them in life or death encounters. Because of this, kata is often referred to as the "Dance of Death."

Over the years, katas have been refined to not only show the power of karate, but also exemplify the beauty and grace that makes it a highly respected art form. When viewing kata, it can easily be compared to a gymnastic floor exercise. Like the gymnast, the karate practitioner must demonstrate the same exceptional balance, speed, power, grace, rhythm, timing, and spirit into his or her performance.

It is the kata that distinguishes one traditional karate style from another by showing the dominant techniques unique to

Master Tatsuo Shimabuku, 10th Dan Red Belt, founder of Isshin Ryu Karate-Do.

that system. For example, the katas of the Okinawan Uechi Ryu system stress hard breathing and few kicks, while the Korean Tang Soo Do forms emphasize many kicks with little hard breathing. If you are enrolled in a traditional karate school, 60 percent of your training will be spent on mastering different katas.

Katas go by a variety of interesting names, given them after the towns they derived from, animals the kata movements resemble, numbers, and their originating master. For example, the eighth empty hand kata in the Isshin Ryu system is called *Sunsu*. Translated it means "Dragon Boy," which was the nickname of Tatsuo Shimabuku, the founder of Isshin Ryu Karate.

The average number of katas required for promotion to black belt can vary anywhere from five to thirty, depending on the style. Because one style has fewer katas than another does not mean it is an inferior system. The fewer katas may be more complicated, with one form equal to three forms of another system.

The different sequences each kata has stem from a variety of combat situations. For example, the techniques of Naihanchi

192

kata—the third in the Isshin Ryu system—are for fighting in a narrow walkway against five opponents, while Kusanku kata of the same system was developed for fighting in a large field at night against fifteen different attackers. Such a mixture of katas gives one the ability to deal with any type of assault.

As a beginner, your first few katas will be very basic, becoming progressively harder as you move up the belt ranks. Much time is spent on kata training because of the immeasurable benefits it has to offer each practitioner. Since katas encompass 90 percent of all karate techniques into a continuous series of moves, they greatly improve a student's stamina, balance, speed, power, concentration, reflexes, timing, focus, rhythm, and spirit. Kata training also teaches self-discipline because of the hard work and dedication needed to perfect its intricate movements. Unlike free fighting, where a partner is required and participation can be limited by age, kata can be practiced individually for years without limitation. To keep fit, masters of old practiced kata on a daily basis well into their 70s and 80s.

Due to the wide variety of karate styles that can be encountered at open tournaments in the United States, empty hand kata competitions are often separated into hard and soft style divisions. Hard styles consist of the Japanese, Okinawan, and Korean schools, while the soft include the Chinese and Indonesian systems. (Only in weapons competition, do contestants of all styles compete in the same ring.)

If you plan on competing, first you must pick a kata you wish to perform regularly in tournaments. As a novice, you may know only one kata, but if you are an advanced belt, you may have as many as twelve forms to choose from. The advice of your instructor will be very valuable at this point. Choose a kata that suits your physical makeup and personality. It must be one you enjoy doing because you will spend many hours perfecting it. Also be careful to choose a form representative of your belt rank. As an experienced kata judge, I can honestly say, officials are not very impressed by brown belts performing yellow belt katas.

It also is wise to have an impressive second kata in your back pocket in case of a tie. If a tie occurs, you will be required to perform a different kata—unless you know only one form—to break the tie. I have often scored a person's second kata higher than his first. This is probably due to his all-out effort to break the tie.

KATA JUDGING

Unlike sparring rules that can vary from tournament to tournament, kata rules and procedures remain constant. They are as follows:

1. All competitors are to wear a complete uniform representative of their style.

2. Competitors will perform in a 20′ × 20′ ropeless ring.

3. When acknowledged to begin their form, competitors must first go before the judges and state their names and the titles of the kata to be performed.

4. Katas will be judged by five black belt officials on a scale of one to ten using full numbers and decimal points. Scores will be shown at the end of each performance; for fairness, the high and low scores will be dropped. If a competitor forgets his kata, he is allowed to start over, but one full point will automatically be dropped from his next score. Kata scoring: 10—perfect; 9—excellent; 8—very good; 7—good; 6—above average; 5—average; 4—below average; 3—fair; 2—poor; 1—very poor; 0—did not complete kata.

5. In case of a tie, the competitors will be asked to perform a different kata to break the tie. If a student knows only one kata, he must repeat the same form for a new score. If the competitors tie a second time, their total scores including the dropped highs and lows will be totaled to determine the winner.

6. Katas will be judged on the following points:

a. Eye contact	e. Balance	i. Rhythm
b. Attitude	f. Control	j. Timing
c. Kiai	g. Speed	k. Stamina
d. Fighting spirit	h. Power	l. Appearance

Your kata scores will be given immediately after your performance.

For competition, your kata should consist of no less than four, well-placed kiais.

Kata movements must be executed with perfect form.

Live the kata.

Strong stances are a must for possessing a winning kata.

KATA WORKOUT ROUTINE

With an average of thirty competitors in your ring, kata competition can be fierce. The only way for your performance to stand out is for you to be in peak physical and mental condition. Kata training requires the same hard work and dedication it takes to be a champion fighter. One need only try to execute three fullpower katas in a row to understand why. This is why I have designed the following workout routine for intermediate and advanced kata students. The workout is required for all members of my competition team three months prior to the tournament season, which begins in March.

Even if you have no interest in competing on a regular basis, the routine can be used as a supplement to your regular kata training. If you find it difficult at first, simply reduce the number of repetitions in the conditioning exercises until your endurance improves. The higher your belt rank, the more difficult the workout will be because of the greater number of katas you will have to perform.

Perform the following exercises in the order shown with as little rest as possible between routines. Working in front of a mirror is important to check your form.

Monday, Wednesday, Friday

1. Prepare yourself for the workout by closing your eyes and going through your favorite kata mentally with the same perfection of movement you would try to achieve in training.

2. Stretch ten minutes.

3. Run two miles.

4. 75 squat jumps.

5. 150 situps.

6. 100 pushups. Do four sets of 25 with a 30-second rest in between sets.

7. In front of a mirror, shadow spar for three minutes to complete warming up the body.

8. Now perform all the katas you know (including weapons katas) for strict form, not power. Walk through them concentrating on eye contact, balance, rhythm, and control.

9. Now execute all katas at full power.

10. Rest five minutes.

11. Execute all forms to be used strictly for competition three times: once for form, once full power, and again for form.

12. End with ten minutes of stretching.

Tuesday and Thursday

1. Stretch ten minutes.
2. Jump rope 15 minutes.
3. Carefully perform all your katas (minus weapons) wearing wrist and ankle weights. Never throw a fullpowered punch or kick wearing these weights because the force can cause injuries to the knees and elbows.
4. Still with weights on, perform all your katas as an isometric exercise. This is done by executing all hand techniques as resistance movements. Punch and block slowly as if trying to move a wall—do not shake when doing so. This conditioning will greatly increase your upper body strength, which should be quite noticeable after three months. All kicks should be executed slowly, holding the leg extended three full seconds before bringing it back to the chamber.
5. Remove the weights and perform all your competition katas in front of fellow students and instructors the way you would at an event. Ask for scores and criticisms about your weak points and suggestions for ways of correcting them.
6. When working on weak points in a kata, there is no need to do the entire form each time. Work the sections that need correcting, then incorporate them back into the entire kata.

INSIDE KATA TIPS

1. Avoid lining up next to a fellow student once your kata ring has been called. For your form to stand out more, it should follow unrelated katas.
2. Your kata should consist of at least four kiais. It is wise to execute your first and last strikes using a kiai, with the other two placed in the middle. Kiais add strength to your form and help draw the attention of the judges.
3. A sign of good control and concentration is to end your katas as near as possible to where you started.
4. If you forget your form or accidentally mix it with another,

do not—under any circumstances—stop your performance. Complete it no matter how it turns out, with the same attitude you would have had had you done it correctly. With so many judges from different styles at open tournaments, there's a good chance some of them won't catch your mistake—you may be shocked at the decent scores you receive. This is a better way to go than starting over, where you will automatically be deducted a full point.

5. Don't start your kata with your body cold and stiff. Warm up for ten minutes prior to your start.

6. At all times, keep your eyes on your imaginary opponent. Never look off at the judges or audience or down at the floor.

7. To perform a kata is to live the kata. See the imaginary attackers coming at you: put your life on the line and act accordingly. Think about it: how would you block, kick, and punch if attacked in real life. It is doubtful you would hold back. The same holds true for kata.

8. As a kata judge, the first things I look for are a student's appearance and attitude. You should have a well-tailored uniform used strictly for tournaments. When presenting yourself before the officials, your attitude should be very respectful by standing at attention, and by beginning your form and leaving your ring after permission has been acknowledged by the head official.

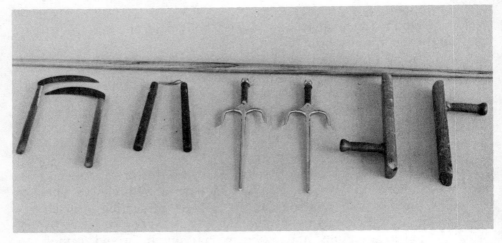

Ancient weaponry (left to right, top to bottom): the bo, the kama, the nunchuku, the sai, and the tonfa.

chapter thirteen

ancient weaponry

Since the display of ancient weaponry has become a regular event at American tournaments, it has become very popular among competitors and spectators alike. One need only witness the beauty and spectacular movements of these weapons performed by skilled experts to understand why.

Weapons training is most often associated with the Chinese and Okinawan karate systems, where mastery of certain weapons is required for a student's advancement to higher belt ranks. The weapons presented here are representative of the Okinawan karate systems.

In the early 1900s Okinawans began incorporating various weapons into their karate systems as a supplement to their regular training, and to preserve their historical art. Okinawan weaponry is referred to as *kobujitsu*, which developed during periods of Okinawan history when all weapons were banned from the island by ruling warlords. To compensate for their loss of protection, the inventive Okinawans turned to what was at hand, which included simple farm implements such as the bo, nunchuku, kama, tonfa, and, with exceptions, the sai.

Bo. Probably the world's oldest known weapon; the *bo* is a rounded, six-foot staff made of hardwood with an average diameter of 3½ inches. The Okinawans usually carried the bo across their shoulders to transport supplies hanging from baskets attached to each end. When attacked, the farmer could slide his loads off and be ready to do combat. The ends of the bo are used to stab and thrust into the attacker's groin, solar plexus, eyes, and throat, while its long length is used to block the entire body against counterstrikes. A person skilled in the bo today could effectively defend himself against a knife-wielding attacker by picking up a simple, everyday instrument such as a mop or broom.

Bo

Nunchuku wards off
a deadly knife attack.

Nunchuku. Popularized by martial arts movies, the nunchuku is kobujitsu's best-known weapon. An easy weapon to conceal, the *nunchuku,* or "chucks" as they are commonly referred to, consist of two 18-inch octangular pieces of hardwood connected by a 4-inch rope or chain. First used by farmers to beat grains, the nunchukus are performed by holding one of the sticks by the end and whipping the free stick out at great speeds. By holding both handles it can also be used to block, choke, and hold your attacker by twisting the cord around the wrist.

Kama. The *kama* is a razor-sharp sickle with a half-moon blade and wooden handle. Used by farmers to cut rice and grass, the kama was used mainly as a defensive weapon against swords and bo attacks. This ancient weapon is still used today by farmers throughout the Japanese and Okinawan countrysides.

Kama

The wooden tonfa blocks and counters the deadly samurai sword.

Tonfa. First used as the handle of a soybean grinder, the *tonfa* is made of white oak, 17 inches in length, 2 inches thick, and with a 5-inch handle near each end. Its thick, wooden base was laid across the forearms to block against other weapons such as a sword or bo, while the blunt end was used to thrust into the attacker's chest or head. It's also used to whip out at the attacker's knee or temple.

Sai. Although not a farm instrument, the sai was used by the Okinawans to defend against the razor-sharp samurai sword. First developed in China and improved upon by the Okinawans,

The sai, Okinawa's most sophisticated weapon, is used to block a bo strike to the knee.

the *sai* is a short, hand-held sword made of steel. It consists of a rounded or octangular blade that is approximately 16 inches in length and a two-pronged wristguard. The sai is kobujitsu's most sophisticated and lethal weapon. It can be used in a variety of ways. The pointed end is used for stabbing and slashing, the blunt handle for punching, the long blade for blocking, and the pronged guard for flipping and hooking the attacker's ankle, groin, or neck. Early warriors also kept a third sai in their belt which they used for throwing at their opponent. The sai and similar *jutte* (one-pronged sai) are still used today by Okinawan and Japanese police to hold back crowds and subdue criminals by applying pressure to certain nerves and joints.

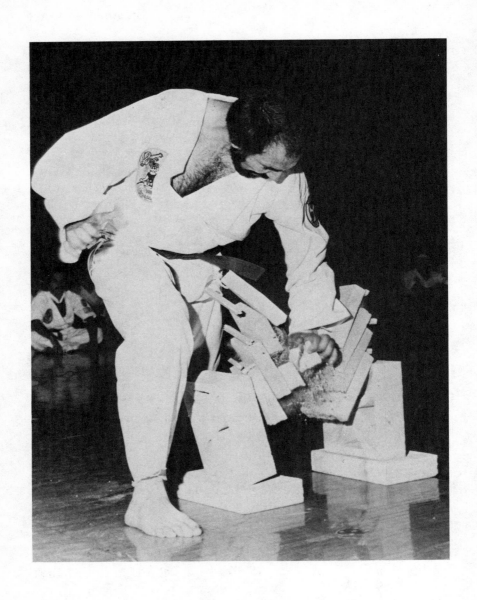

chapter fourteen

breaking and other feats

To observe a karate expert smashing through stacks of bricks and wood with his bare hands and feet is truly an amazing sight. Although breaking encompasses only about 5 percent of a student's training, it is generally viewed by the uneducated public as the only thing karate consists of.

Breaking was developed as a means of testing a karateka's mental concentration and striking power. One need only witness a side kick smashing through four one-inch boards to realize the effect it would have on an attacker's rib cage. Although this feat is practiced infrequently, knowledge of breaking is important because most schools of karate require it as part of black belt exams.

BREAKING TECHNIQUES

How is it possible for someone to strike his hand or foot into an object that is harder than his own body without injuring himself? The answer lies not so much in one's size and strength, but rather in his technique and conditioning.

Before a student attempts breaking, he or she should hold the rank of a green or brown belt. At these levels a student possesses the necessary discipline, balance, speed, and confidence needed to break something successfully. The body also has to be conditioned in a special way by training regularly on the *makiwara* (striking post). By striking the makiwara, tough calluses develop on the hands and feet which protect the striking areas from abrasive injuries.

When breaking, it is of utmost importance that you choose the proper materials. Wood should be grade two pine, one inch thick and one foot square, and free of knots. Woods other than grade two pine are virtually impossible to break when more than one piece is used. Bricks and cinder blocks should be untempered and of the patio kind. Be sure to keep your material dry. Water binds wood and cement, allowing it less give, which can cause injuries.

For toughening the outside edge of your hands, stand to the side of the makiwara in a front stance. Keeping the striking hand open with the fingers tensed tightly together and thumb down, swing your hand from the back shoulder into the target. When making contact, rub your hand back and forth in a sawing motion two times for greater callus development. Work up to where you can do 50 repetitions daily with each hand.

When straight punching the makiwara, stand in a front stance with the target lined up with your solar plexus. Begin by holding the nonstriking hand out just to the side of the target. As you punch the pad, pull your outstretched arm into your hip for added power. Repeat this alternating technique for every strike. Be sure to make contact with only the two large top knuckles of the striking hand. Perform 50 repetitions daily with each hand.

To toughen the feet for breaking, strike the makiwara with the ball of the foot by keeping the toes pulled back and the foot straight as shown. Besides executing front kicks, also practice hitting it with the blade by executing side kicks and the heel by performing back kicks. Strike the makiwara with 25 repetitions of each kick daily.

210

The following techniques apply to all breaking whether performed with the hand or foot. The crossover, side-thrust kick directed at four one-inch boards and at midsection height will act as a model. (As a beginner with an average body weight of 150 pounds, two boards should prove to be sufficient. Breaking bricks should not be attempted until you have reached the rank of brown or black belt.)

1. When setting up your break, have two assistants hold the boards at the corners with their arms locked straight out. Make sure the grain of the wood is aligned by your holders in the same direction as the strike.

2. Determine your distance and focus point by measuring your kick so the foot will end up four inches beyond the target when your leg is fully extended. As mentioned in the beginning of this book, proper placement of focus point will eliminate weak surface hitting.

3. After the proper distance has been determined, begin to psych yourself up to eliminate any fears or doubts you may have. One way of doing this is to look at the boards as being a vicious attacker who must be stopped with one kick. This type of thinking will give you power you never knew you had.

SIDE KICK BREAK. Distancing is too close to the boards; leg will be jammed, causing loss of power.

211

Focusing too far away will cause ineffective surface hitting; there is not enough force to go through all four pieces.

Perfect distancing: There is enough bend in the leg to drive the foot through all the pieces.

212

THE BREAK. After having executed two practice runs to gauge the proper distance for the final break, face the boards in a side stance with your guard up and with breathing relaxed.

To break with the crossover side kick, step forward, with your back leg crossing behind the front and point your hip at the target.

Bring your lead leg up high into the chamber, keeping the foot in the blade position. At all times, keep your eyes on the target.

Complete the break by exploding your foot through the center of the boards. Remember when a break is performed, the entire sequence of movements should be done quickly without hesitation.

KARATE FEATS (MIND OVER MATTER)

After many years of training in karate a person can reach such a high level of physical conditioning and mental control that he or she is capable of performing feats that seem quite impossible. Through the daily practice of meditation and ancient sanchin breathing exercises, the body can become as hard as stone and impervious to certain types of pain. *Sanchin* is an isometric-type exercise performed by inhaling air through the nose, down to the lower abdomen, and forced out the mouth. This hard breathing, which is a trademark of the Okinawan karate systems, is coordinated with upper-body resistance exercises. When the mind and body come together in the hard sanchin state, a practitioner is capable of taking blows from his attacker with little or no injury. The following feats demonstrate the degree of punishment the body is capable of withstanding when applying the sanchin breathing technique. These feats take years to master, and should never be attempted by an inexperienced karateka.

The author performing sanchin kata, the oldest known kata in karate. With the feet turned in tightly, air is taken in through the nose, down to the lower abdomen, and forced hard out the mouth, as all muscle groups are tensed. This ancient training technique gives the body an inner strength, commonly referred to as *ki*. The coordination of the breathing techniques with the proper hand and foot movements takes many years to master.

215

A steel-tipped arrow can be pushed into the throat until it breaks, without injury.

To show the conditioning effect that hard sanchin breathing has on the body, a 6-foot-long, 2" × 2" beam is smashed over the author's arm. Applying sanchin to a real self-defense situation could have the same effect when blocking a lethal club attack.

As a challenge to himself, an experienced karateka may wish to attempt feats designed to test his mental and physical abilities.

breaking and other feats

Bed of razor-sharp nails.

A demonstration of one's *ki:* Lying on a bed of nails as six, 2"-thick cement slabs are smashed on the stomach.

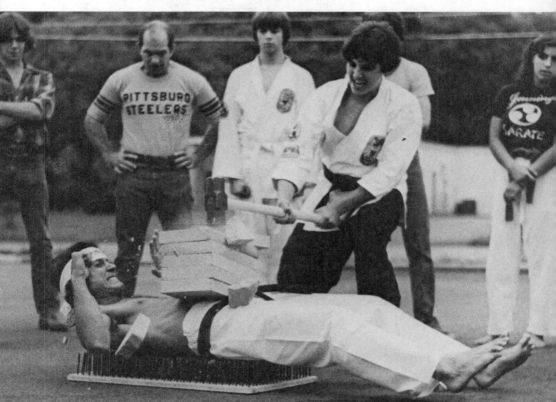

chapter fifteen

a final kiai-finding
a good karate school

I have been fortunate throughout my karate career to have studied under some of the finest teachers in the world. These were dedicated people who not only taught the physical aspects of karate, but also the important mental aspects of control, courtesy, discipline, and respect. After all, these virtues are what the martial arts are built on.

I am sure that if you are not currently enrolled in a school, you will want to seek one out as your interest in karate grows. Before you run out and sign up at the nearest *dojo* (training hall), I feel there are some very important points you should consider when choosing a school and an instructor.

Begin by making a list of all the available schools in your area, of which the majority can be found in the Yellow Pages of

219

your phone directory. Do not be taken in by the size of the ads and all the wonders they proclaim their schools can accomplish for you. Call each studio and set up an appointment to meet with the director and to observe a class. It also is a good idea to request a free trial lesson. If a school refuses to honor any of these requests, disregard it immediately. Never put down your hard-earned money unless you know exactly what you're paying for.

Upon entering a school, look over the facility thoroughly. It should be well-equipped with a spacious workout area and radiate cleanliness, which is a sign of pride. Inquire as to whether the school is a full- or part-time operation. A full-time school is usually a better choice because it can offer the student longer operating hours and more flexible class times.

The head *Sensei* (teacher) should not approach you with a hard sell when you meet him. If he acts as though his only interest is to get you to sign on the dotted line, look elsewhere. A quality teacher is one who is looking out for your best interests. He should show his concern for you by taking the time to discuss your reasons for wanting to study karate, and how he and his school can help you fulfill your goals. He should also be honest and realistic about your expected progress. If he fills your head with promises of making you a black belt expert within a year, no matter what your abilities, he is giving away belts with little concern about developing your full potential. In most schools of karate, it takes an average of four years and up to achieve the rank of black belt. Never take the easy road to belt advancement. Study with the goal of being a respected karateka, deserving, and able to back up your belt ranks.

During your interview, do not be afraid to ask the instructor these very important questions. How long has he been studying and teaching his art? What makes him qualified to teach? Who did he study under and can his teacher be contacted as a reference to his abilities? What degrees does he hold and who awarded them? What did he have to do to receive these degrees? What is the background and history of his system? What does his style emphasize in training? What, if any, organizations does he belong to? How long has he been in business at the present location? Has he ever operated another school? The *Sensei* should be open to your questions and happy to answer them. If not, he obviously has something to hide and should be doubted. In reference to the last question, I personally feel a good school is one that has been operating successfully in the community for seven or more years and run by an instructor with as many years teaching experience.

After you have concluded your discussion, do not enroll without observing a class. By watching a training session you will be able to judge the sincerity of the claims made by the school director, and to evaluate the quality of instruction. It will also give you an opportunity to observe the relationship between students and teachers. Good or bad, whatever you witness will be a reflection of the head *Sensei*.

If the students are allowed to goof-off and seem to lack the abilities of their belt ranks, the school lacks professionalism and high standards. There should be a comfortable feeling of seriousness and mutual respect between students and teachers. The instructors should stress control and make it a point to remind the class that karate is used only as a last resort. Avoid instructors who parade around the floor like a drill sergeant barking commands with such strictness that the students feel uncomfortable and almost afraid to breathe. A good teacher is one who will come across as firm yet compassionate to the students' needs, ready to help whenever asked.

More important than the physical aspects of karate are the teachings of respect, courtesy, and control, which all true martial arts are built on.

the last kiai—finding a good karate school

Once you have decided on a school and instructor to suit your standards and needs, a big commitment on your part must then be made. Besides your monthly financial obligation, which can run anywhere from $20 to $60 a month depending on the facility and number of classes you take, you will be expected to attend classes no less than two days a week, along with putting in extra time at home. I suggest you enroll for no less than one year so you can truly benefit from the karate training.

I hope I have given you some valuable insight into finding a good school, but you must remember, the finest facility and greatest *Sensei* in the world is worthless without the dedication and hard-working effort of the student. Good luck and train hard.

karate terms

The following words are frequently used in Japanese and Okinawan karate schools:

General Terms

Empty Hand: *Karate*
Contest: *Shiai*
Meditation: *Mokuso*
Bow: *Rei*
Begin: *Hajime*
Attention: *Kiotsuke*
Teacher: *Sensei*
Training Hall: *Dojo*
Opponent: *Aite*
Sparring: *Kumite*
Technique: *Waza*
Uniform: *Gi*
Belt: *Obi*
Yell: *Kiai*
Focus: *Kime*
Style: *Ryu*
Grade: *Dan*
Black Belt: *Sho Dan*
Form: *Kata*
Thank You: *Arigato*
Breaking: *Tamashiari*
Strike: *Uchi*
Stance: *Dachi*
Student: *Karateka*
Headband: *Hachimaka*
Seated Position: *Sazen*
Master Instructor: *Shihan*

Kicks

Front Kick: *Mae Geri*
Side Kick: *Yoko Geri*
Back Kick: *Ushiro Geri*
Roundhouse Kick: *Mawashi Geri*
Stomp Kick: *Ushiro Fumikomi*
Crescent Kick: *Mikazuki Geri*
Knee Kick: *Hisa Geri*
Hook Kick: *Kake Geri*
Flying Side Kick: *Tobi Yoko Geri*

Counting One to Ten

One: *Ichi*
Two: *Ni*
Three: *San*
Four: *Shi*
Five: *Go*
Six: *Roku*
Seven: *Shichi*
Eight: *Hachi*
Nine: *Ku*
Ten: *Ju*

Stances

Front Stance: *Seisan Dachi*

Cat Stance: *Neko Ashi Dachi*
Horse Stance: *Shiko Dachi*
Leaning Back Stance: *Kokutsu Dachi*
Attention: *Masubi Dachi*

Parts of the Foot

Ball: *Koshi*
Heel: *Kakato*
Instep: *Haisoku*
Blade: *Sokuto*
Arch: *Achi*

Parts of the Hand

Backfist Punch: *Uraken*
Forefist Punch: *Seiken*
Hammer Fist: *Kentsui*
Knife Hand: *Shuto*
Palm Heel: *Teisho*
Ridge Hand: *Haito*
Spear Hand: *Nukite*
Elbow: *Empi*
Four-Knuckle Fist: *Hiraken*

index